ONLINE POKER

ONLINE POKER

**Your Guide to Playing Online Poker
Safely & Winning Money!**

Cardoza Publishing

DOYLE
BRUNSON

Cardoza Publishing is the foremost gaming publisher in the world, with a library of over 175 up-to-date and easy-to-read books and strategies. These authoritative works are written by the top experts in their fields and with more than 8,500,000 books in print, represent the best-selling and most popular gaming books anywhere.

FIRST EDITION

Copyright © 2005 by Doyle Brunson

- All Rights Reserved -

Library of Congress Catalog Card No: 2003113828
ISBN: 1-58042-132-6

Visit our web site—www.cardozapub.com—or write for a full list of books and computer strategies.

CARDOZA PUBLISHING
P.O. Box 1500, Cooper Station, New York, NY 10276
Phone (800) 577-WINS
email: cardozapub@aol.com
www.cardozapub.com

ABOUT THE AUTHOR

Doyle Brunson is the "Babe Ruth of Poker," a living legend who still plays in the highest limit poker games in the world. Along the way, winning more money at poker than any man who has ever lived, he won back-to-back world championships in 1976 and 1977 and a total of nine WSOP gold bracelets—no player has more.

Doyle's latest victories gave him the unique distinction of winning gold bracelets in four decades—the 70's, 80's, 90's and 00's—an accomplishment that may never be matched. In late August 2004, Doyle competed against and won against the largest field ever to play a World Poker Tour event, 667 players, making him the first player to win a WSOP and WPT title.

Doyle is also the author of *Poker Wisdom of a Champion*, the original *Super/System*, hailed by professionals as the most influential poker book ever written and still considered the "bible" of poker, and its fabulous companion volume, *Super/System 2*.

♠♥♦♣

Table of Contents

Introduction

This book provides my most profitable advice—including detailed examples—of how you should approach the game of poker on the Internet.

Because the main premises that make poker profitable remain constant, whether you're playing in private games, real-world casinos, or online, I will only give important general strategy tips that apply across the board. Emphasis will be given to what makes online poker *different*.

And, believe me, it *is* different. If you're an accomplished player who takes advantage of face-to-face psychological domination to use a super aggressive style of play, let me give you a word of caution: *You aren't going to win that way online*. You can play aggressively online, and often you should, but you can't play aggressively in the same way. Sorting out when to do it and when not to do it makes all the difference between winning and losing. And I'll help you do that.

Poker is the greatest game on earth, and the only one where you can win a pot on raw aggression, even if you don't have the best hand—just because you have the courage to bet. It's the only game where skill eventually reigns in the illusion of luck as certainly as the sun will rise in the morning.

And I invite you to begin this adventure online. For me, playing poker by aiming my cursor and clicking on my mouse or trackball has been a thrill I could never have dreamed of when I was traveling the dusty Texas circuit back in the sixties. Having had that early experience, my mind is quick to make comparisons between that kind of poker and the kind I play at live tables in Las Vegas and the modern miracle of online poker. But, making these comparisons gives me valuable insight into how to adapt.

So, let's begin to get you familiar with the idea of playing poker online, to show the advantages and disadvantages, and to show you how to be a winning online player!

♠♥♦♣

A Word About Doyle

— by Mike Caro —

There is no other competitor like Doyle Brunson. It doesn't matter what the game is. It doesn't need to be poker. If you can play it and beat it, he probably can play it and beat it better. And if he thinks he can, he'll gamble with you—and sooner or later he *will* find a way to win your money.

The legendary back-to-back world poker champion Doyle Brunson—the man who's won more championship bracelets at the World Series of Poker than anyone in history[1]—has now become the primary advocate for on-line poker. His stature as the world's leading poker player hasn't been in doubt for almost 40 years, but it wasn't until the publication of *Doyle Brunson's Super/System—A Course in Power Poker* in 1978, that he redefined the game and became regarded as a poker visionary.

Using his unparalleled prestige to convince the other top five players in the world, each a specialist in his own form of poker, to cooperate, he was able to show once and for all that the skill aspect of poker prevails. And he shared his knowledge and that of his "expert collaborators" with the public. This single event is often credited as the spark that brought poker out of the dark ages and into the spotlight.

Now he lends his name to something equally visionary. It's a *new* vision. Part of poker is moving online to the Internet. And that may be the primary arena for poker in the years ahead. Realizing this, Doyle Brunson has lent his name to an online poker site, DoylesRoom.com, and has become a primary advocate for the advancement and the integrity of Internet play.

When I first saw Doyle Brunson in action at a poker table in 1977, I was astonished. We'd played in different worlds. My world was in Gardena, California, where five-card draw poker was the only form of poker played, by state law. The city put a maximum on bet sizes—$20. So, it was unusual to win or lose more than $2,500 in a day. That wasn't a fortune, even back then. Doyle's world was Las Vegas, where hold'em and seven-card stud ruled. You couldn't even find a draw poker game in Las Vegas. And when Doyle played, it was for *big* money. You *could* win or lose a fortune in a single day.

And here I was watching hold'em for the first time ever. I'd never played it. It was thrilling. Doyle wasn't just beating these games, he was *conquering* them. *Owning* them. *Mangling* them. He'd bluff so casually, almost always at the perfect time, and he'd get away with the pot. Watching him play was like watching a masterpiece being painted.

BIG LEAGUE POKER

I may never have gotten to see this phenomenal play close up had Doyle not decided I was the world's best draw player and selected me to contribute a section to *Super/System*. That honor brought me to Las Vegas, and I was seeing truly big league poker for the first time. And I was privileged to hang around with the king of poker. Doyle Brunson. The man who had just won his second world championship in a row. *Texas Dolly*. And seeing him play opened my eyes and stretched my horizons. I don't think I would have fully evolved into the Mike Caro you know today if I hadn't had the good fortune to see Doyle play almost 30 years ago.

Pot after pot, decision after decision, he was right on target. I had never seen anything like it at the time, I haven't seen anything like it since, and I don't expect to see anything like it in the future—except, possibly, from Doyle himself.

NEW INSIGHTS

In this book, Doyle shares his poker wisdom by introducing us to a new world of play—online poker. He's endorsed a magnificent site called DoylesRoom.com. His vision in this arena is so monumental that I no longer endorse any other sites. Doyle's Room is my room, and I think you should consider making it your room when you're playing online.

As you might imagine, consulting on a cyberspace casino gave Doyle new insights. And, as always, he's eager to pass them along. The book you're holding fills yet another gap in poker publishing—thanks once again to Doyle Brunson.

But his unrivaled poker expertise, skill, and vision aren't the only reason I'm proud to call Doyle Brunson a friend. There's much more to his character than that. I shared it in a forward I wrote for his book: *According to Doyle* since retitled to *Poker Wisdom of a Champion.* I'd like you to read it now…

"Let me tell you something that happened in 1980 that speaks to the extraordinary character of Doyle Brunson. Three years earlier, Doyle had established a business to produce his acclaimed strategy book, *Doyle Brunson's Super/System—A Course in Power Poker…* When the project was finished, he dismantled the company and placed an honest young woman in charge of the remaining business.

"Left for a year without supervision, something happened. She developed a slot machine habit, continually losing her wages. When her income couldn't sustain her, she began desperately "borrowing" money from the company, while trying to keep the records credible.

"You could tell how hurt Doyle was when he found out. I didn't know what to expect. Would he call the police?

"I remember that he sat at his desk and took a deep breath, as if he were scrutinizing a large pot. Then he looked directly into her eyes. Soft-spoken as always, using his soothing Texas drawl, Doyle said, "I know you didn't mean to do it. Nobody feels worse about this than you do, so I guess it won't do me any good to holler. Sometimes people do things without really knowing why. Deep down, you're still an honest person.

"We drove her to the Sahara Hotel in Las Vegas, and because she was broke, Doyle handed her $100. Just before she crossed the street and entered the club, he said, 'When you get your head straight, come on back and I'll write you up a recommendation.'

"Doyle, a former athlete, is very tall and heavy (at that time). But, it wasn't until then that I truly understood the size of this man. His advice, much like his character, speaks for itself."

[1]Mike Caro, "the Mad Genius of Poker," is the world's foremost authority on poker strategy, psychology, and statistics. He is the founder of Mike Caro University of Poker, which can be found online at www.poker1.com.

The New World of Poker

Between the sudden surge of televised poker and on-line poker, more new players have been exposed to our game than ever before in history. And it helps everyone. The real-world casinos are flooded with new players. Did you ever think poker would get this hot? I didn't. It's a fantasy come true.

I believe many potential players, who otherwise would feel too embarrassed to walk through the front doors of a public casino to play poker against more-experienced opponents, will find that courage now that they can play their first hands on the Internet. And if it weren't for the Internet, poker wouldn't be as popular or as carefully analyzed. Sometimes a man needs to lean back in his chair and picture how things would be under other circumstances. Only then does it become clear what factors were most important in getting us where we are today.

TELEVISED POKER AND ITS IMPACT

Now, clearly, the trend toward televised poker has had a great deal to do with our game's growing popularity. Specifically, the advent of tiny "lipstick" cameras and "under the table" cameras have played a major part in making these telecasts more intriguing. Poker had been televised for years, and it did find a loyal following. But it didn't really boom until those non-intrusive cameras were able to relay the secret cards to the viewing audience. Before that, you had to guess what a player might be holding.

To be sure, you could argue—and some players *did* argue—that showing the hands would make the telecasts *less* popular! They reasoned that it would take away the suspense. I sure didn't think so. I thought that, while it would destroy the suspense of wondering what a player might have *in* a hand, it would build suspense based on what a player might do *with* a hand. And that's exactly what happened.

There's something fascinating about knowing what all the players hold and watching how the play unfolds. You know something the players *don't* know. Even for seasoned professionals like me, the innovation added a whole new aspect to the game. Poker became truly a magnificent spectator sport, simply by adding a new dimension to the game that was geared specifically to those watching. In fact, this advance made televised poker so popular that the World Poker Tour is now the most watched program on the Travel Channel—its home base.

And I hear that on ESPN, poker is more watched than any other televised event except NFL football and some of the major league baseball games.

That's saying a lot. No wonder the major networks are now focusing on poker. And I know of many more network telecasts in the works. That's the contribution television made to poker in the last few years—turning it into a popular spectator sport. That's a turn of events few envisioned.

ONLINE POKER USHERS IN A NEW ERA

But while television did a great deal to build interest by making poker a spectator event *and* one that could be played without traditional athletic skills, the sudden surge of online poker lowered the entry bar for millions of new players and launched the game into the modern age.

The reason players flocked to the game was mostly due to the fact that poker was easily accessible for the first time in world history. Sure, you could play in your own home before this, but in order to do that, *others* had to come visit. You had to make space available, maybe prepare snacks, and if not enough players showed up, you had no game. And, of course, when they went home—because they went broke, got tired, or got rich—you had no game any longer. You just had a mess to clean up.

Worse, it was no *convenience* having a poker game at home. It was an *inconvenience*. I suppose people playing poker games at homes with friends and relatives always hoped they wouldn't be the one to have to play host. So,

I can't tell you that you've never been able to play poker from your home without traveling before, but I can tell you that Internet poker is a whole new ballgame.

Just think about it. You used to have to dress right, go to a casino or find a lucrative game far down the road. Today, you can just sit in your favorite computer chair or pop a notebook computer in your lap anywhere, and you're playing poker! Nobody has to deal, no arguments about betting, and if you're new to the game, you don't have to worry about fumbling with cards, knowing when it's your turn to act, or figuring out if your cards are strong enough to win the pot in a showdown. The computer does all this for you!

When I was a kid in Texas, I just couldn't possibly have imagined that this would all come to be. Nobody could. And what a way to break into the poker world. It's like playing for matchsticks as a first poker experience—as some used to do—but without even having to handle the matchsticks or the cards. If you want new players to discover poker without stress, this has to be the miracle of all poker miracles. The Internet! Sometimes I shake my head just thinking about it. On one hand, it seems so strange to me that it actually happened, but on the other hand, I'm getting so used to it that I'm starting to take it for granted.

Isn't progress something?

THE MAGIC OF TECHNOLOGY

Technology surrounds us. Things change. And the swiftness of change today is unparalleled in history. Nothing makes poker players more aware of this change than the advent of online poker. It used to be, centuries ago, that not much was different from decade to decade. In fact, life was pretty much the same century after century.

Then came the industrial age. Machines began to take the drudgery out of some jobs. But, still, big inventions were rare and it took a lot of time for them to be adopted. So, even as modern progress gained momentum, you could still be Rip Van Winkle, asleep for 25 years. When you woke up, the world would still be recognizable and you could function in it.

Then, in the last hundred years, everything became unhinged. New inventions flew into our lives one after another until each 25 years made life completely different. Radios. Movies. Automobiles. Airplanes. Jet planes. Moon landings. Television. High definition television. Record players. Cassette tapes. CD audio. Audio recorders. Video recorders. Camcorders. Video tape movies. DVD movies. On and on. And, yes, computers.

Computers changed everything, from research, to productivity, to games. Poker, too. You see, along came the Internet and suddenly you could find almost any answer in seconds, be anywhere in the world, instantly—not physically, of course, but we learned we didn't need to be physically present to be there.

And so we could play poker without being physically present. We could be at the table. Instantly.

I remember the first time I played poker online was in 1999. I think it was a tiny $3 limit game and I was used to playing $2,000 limit and higher games where you could win or lose upwards of $1 million without leaving your seat. I'd gotten curious, because Mike Caro had endorsed an online poker site, and I thought this was strange, considering he had previously written a column warning of the pitfalls of online play. If he'd changed his mind, then the least I could do was investigate for myself. Remarkably, it was as exciting as any poker I'd ever played. Just the fact that I was participating in poker on the screen with opponents seated inches away, but knowing they weren't actually inches away. They were in England and Germany and Hong Kong. Everywhere. I was playing poker in a game that could never have been possible before.

A TORNADO

And so, unexpected and out of nowhere, online poker blew onto the scene. It was like a tornado sweeping down the Texas Panhandle. And I realized—grudgingly at first—that online poker was here to stay. You could now put poker into two main categories: *online* poker and *real-world* poker. Notice that I'm saying "real-world" poker, not "real" poker. That's because online poker *was* real poker. It was certainly real for the hundreds of thousands of new players around the world who were playing for *real* money! In fact, what is there about online poker that makes it *un*real? Not much, and that's why I think most have us have started differentiating poker by just these two terms: *online* poker and *real-world* poker.

And real-world poker, the kind you sit down and play with physical cards at a real table against opponents you can reach across the table and shake hands with, can itself be divided into subcategories. For instance, we could talk about *home* poker and *casino* poker. Each offers a slightly different flavor. That's the same with basketball, you know. There is basketball played outdoors on concrete slabs, high school basketball, college basketball, NBA basketball, and international basketball that you see in the Olympics. But it's all basketball.

And I'm here to tell you that, online or real-world, poker is poker. It's *all* poker. There's hardly any advice on these pages that won't help you become a much better online player, simply because it will help you to become a much better poker player, period.

DOYLE'S ROOM ONLINE (WWW.DOYLESROOM.COM)

Before I discuss some of the powerful techniques that will help you win at online poker, I want to tell you something that may surprise you. The truth is, it surprises me, because not too many years ago, I couldn't imagine myself being involved in online poker at all. Briefly, I got myself talked into endorsing a friend's start-up website, but I extricated myself from that fiasco as soon as I realized that only the big boys can afford to play in this business. Chalk it up as another of my bad ventures when trying to help others out.

Well, now I got smart. If you have a computer and want to know how smart, check out www.doylesroom.com for actual play in practice games—and beyond! And for other things poker, try www.doylesroom.net. While I don't have any ownership, nor do I participate in management, I'm glad they're putting my name on it—because they're paying me a handsome endorsement fee, and because it's a site that makes me proud of my association.

Using the site that they've put my name on, doylesroom.com, as an example of what online poker looks like today, I'll walk you through some examples of how that ever-growing form of poker is played. Remember, by the time you read this, doylesroom.com—and other competing sites—may be even more advanced. I envision being able to bet just by speaking and scrutinizing live, moving images of your opponents, bringing the most sorely missed element of traditional poker to the online world—tells.

TODAY AND YESTERDAY

Besides playing the World Series of Poker nearly every year—which, in 2005, was moved from Binion's Horseshoe to the Rio to accommodate the larger fields of players—I've found temporary homes at the Mirage and the Bellagio in Las Vegas. Years ago, it was the Silver Bird (which I actually helped run for a short time twenty-five years ago) and the Dunes—and others. Sadly, neither the Silver Bird nor the Dunes exist today.

I guess that's progress, but when these two casinos tumbled to the ground to make room for new mega-casinos, many of my fondest memories tumbled away with them. Memories blowing away like tumbleweeds across the Texas Panhandle. For a moment they were right in front of me, plain as plain can be. And then they grew more and more distant, until I now have to reach far back in my mind to remember the glory of those moments and those long-ago days when I chased games—few and far between—down the highways of Texas and the South.

THE GROWTH OF POKER

In 2004, I was honored to be inducted into the Poker Walk of Fame at the Commerce Casino, near Los Angeles. Have you ever visited that casino? It's the biggest physical cardroom in the world. There are hundreds of poker tables! In my whole life as a poker player, I never envisioned that there would ever be fifty games going under one roof, let alone hundreds. And Commerce isn't the only major poker room to host a huge number of poker tables. In the Los Angeles area, there's also the Bicycle Casino and the Hustler. These are three casinos where I enjoy playing poker.

In Las Vegas, where I have lived for more than thirty years, poker rooms seem to be opening up everywhere with casino after casino, needing to stay competitive, offering this great game to their patrons. And poker is not just limited to the West. Jack Binion launched large-scale poker rooms in the Midwest, and there are now big rooms on the East Coast, too, including Foxwoods in Connecticut and inside several casinos in Atlantic City. Poker is booming everywhere.

But put those all together, and you have maybe 1,000 tables. The tremendous growth in the number of poker games available and the cardrooms in which to play them, is something I never imagined when I was starting my career going from one single-table private game to another.

When you play real-world poker today, you have to travel to find the right games. However, when you play poker online, you're within instant reach of any table. A few clicks of your mouse and you're at another table, maybe at the same online casino, maybe at another.

The one thing that will shock you the most is the number of poker players currently online. Just how many tables are we talking about? You'll often find over 7,000 real-money tables going online at the same time— some tournament tables, some regular ring games.

Most days there will be over 50,000 real-money players that you can choose to play against without leaving your home. And then there are the free, practice games, and I'd hesitate to count how many players and tables there are of those.

So while I am often found playing poker in the high stakes games of Las Vegas or wherever I may be on the road, I always have a home base—a place to go regularly when there's nothing to draw me somewhere else. For me, it's Doyle's Room, and I hope you'll make it your home base, too.

Where to Play, Learn, & Discuss Poker Online

You now can discover poker, learn the rules, and get familiar with the procedures without even risking a penny! That's because almost all major poker sites on the Web offer free practice games as a way to introduce online poker to the budding poker community.

I believe there are many millions of new players today who would never have played the game regularly had it not been for the advent of online poker. But, if you're going to play online, you might as well play smart. And that's why I wrote this book.

Before you can play well, or play at all, I suppose you need to know where to play. I'm about to give you some choices, but—with the exception of Doyle's Room—I'm not saying which are the best. And these aren't the only places, either. They're just the ones I'm most familiar with, ones that come easily to mind.

It wouldn't be prudent for me to make an extensive list anyway because by the time this book got to press and in your hands, new sites would have come alive and a few old, underfinanced or uncompetitive ones might have folded their doors. Some might even have changed names or merged. So, remember, this is just a list to get you started on your quest. I hope you'll visit me at Doyle's Room, where you'll often see me join in the games just to socialize. Other noted players will do that from time to time at Doyle's Room too, especially Mike Caro, who endorses my room and plays regularly under his own name.

If you're eager to get started, let's see what some of your choices are.

LIST OF PLACES TO PLAY POKER

There are hundreds of online poker rooms—and the number is growing every month. Most are small endeavors that never seem to attract enough players to prosper, and as a result, many of them fail. That's why I think you should stick to the most prominent ones with proven records or those backed by people you trust. The list of sites you see here isn't complete. It's just some of the sites I know about that you might want to consider.

Naturally, I think Doyle's Room is the best—by a Texas mile. But, from time to time, you may want to test your luck at other online poker rooms, just as you might want to move from cardroom to cardroom in the real world. I'm primarily a poker player, and I know that sometimes you might find the best games at different locations or find a place you're temporarily most comfortable with.

All the sites below offer free practice games, and with the exception of Yahoo, you can play real-money on every one of them.

DOYLE'S ROOM
www.doylesroom.com

It has my name on it. It's a leading member of the Apex Poker Network that includes over 100 sister sites, supplying players from around the globe (including Victor Chandler and Golden Palace) and guaranteeing round-the-clock action.

FULL TILT
www.fulltiltpoker.com

Newer site promoted by some of the leading poker personalities.

LADBROKES
www.ladbrokepoker.com

Primarily a European site, backed by England's most visible name in gaming.

PARADISE POKER
www.paradisepoker.com

One of the earlier and still busier sites.

PARTY POKER
www.partypoker.com
> Currently the largest online poker room.

PLANET POKER
www.planetpoker.com
> The first online real-money site, it debuted in 1997.

POKER STARS
www.pokerstars.com
> An up-and-coming site, featuring lots of tournament action.

ULTIMATE BET
www.ultimatebet.com
> Along with Doyle's Room, Full Tilt, and others, this site adds larger-limit games to its offerings.

YAHOO POKER
http://www.poker.kg/yahoo_poker.html
> No real-money games here, but it's a popular place to practice.

QUICK NOTE ON PLAYING LEGALLY

Whatever you do, make sure your site of choice is legally licensed to operate in the nation where it resides. If you stick to the main entities backed by reputable people you've heard about, you can be fairly certain the site is operating legally.

You also want to make sure that you can legally play. Only you, through a legal consultant or attorney where you live, can determine if it's okay to play. That's because, while the major poker rooms operate legally and are licensed in various countries, it's difficult to know which countries or jurisdictions fully permit their citizens to participate. Remember, however, that all ethical sites forbid minors to play. Since it's impossible for Internet poker rooms to interpret or even know what's legal in literally thousands of jurisdictions throughout the world, they leave it to the player to determine if play is allowed.

It's a shame that some nations aren't so enthusiastic about online poker—some Middle East nations, as an example, are particularly hostile to games where money may be exchanged, even though the skill factor eventually predominates—but despite this, online poker has made the game a worldwide experience. It's not uncommon to see, for example, players from England, France, Australia, Canada, and other nations playing in the same online poker game.

I watch the typed conversations, using the chat feature, among players during the game and realize that long-range friendships are being established that would never before be possible. Poker is the binding force. And the Internet is the vehicle that unleashes it.

It would be a shame if players in the United States, the cultural core of poker, came to be uninvited from the game that is now a global adventure. And, I guess that's all I'm going to say about it for now.

LIST OF PLACES TO LEARN POKER

I guess you could just dive into the poker pond and learn to swim the hard way. The trouble is, you wouldn't be swimming with the fish. You'd be one of the fish—and "fish" isn't a flattering term in poker. It means you're easy to catch and conquer. And you supply nourishment to the bankrolls of superior players.

Now, I grew up in a day and age when it was easier to dive straight into the poker pond, because that was about the only way to get a poker education. This was true for me, but more importantly, it was true for my opponents. They didn't have the luxury of looking strategy up in poker books, either. Most of the poker literature of the day—and there wasn't a lot of it—was hit and miss. There were occasional glimmers of good advice, but most of it was suspect. So, like I said, you learned the hard way. You played.

That's what I did. But, let me tell you, if I had it to do all over again today, I'd make it easier on myself. I'd read and research first—at least before entering games big enough to potentially do me great harm. I might practice in real-money games, putting small sums of money at risk. But I wouldn't put my early bankrolls in jeopardy as recklessly or as often. I recommend you study first and play small until you're comfortable playing larger.

The poker-learning sites listed here are just the ones I'm most familiar with. There are hundreds more, some excellent, some not-so-excellent, and some giving almost comically poor advice. Just as with the poker-playing sites, it wouldn't do me much good to compose a complete list, because new sites would come along and many of the old ones would disappear before this book was published. The ones I've chosen are some of those that I consider useful, accurate, and reliable.

DOYLE'S ROOM
www.doylesroom.net

This poker information and learning site is affiliated with my poker room and has exclusive gateways to Mike Caro University of Poker.

POKER1
www.poker1.com

This is the premier free learning and educational site on the Internet with odds, lessons, articles, videos, audios, whole books, and more. Poker1 is exclusively affiliated with Doyle's Room and the online home to Mike Caro University of Poker.

POKER PAGES
www.pokerpages.com

A treasury of poker news, tournament results, articles, and more. Gateway to Poker School Online.

CARD PLAYER
www.cardplayer.com

Packed with poker news, archives of Card Player magazine columns, and more.

POKER PLAYER
www.pokerplayernewspaper.com

Read the entire contents of all issues of Poker Player newspaper.

PLAY WINNING POKER
www.playwinningpoker.com
Odds, strategy, and a lot of thoughtful information.

AVERY CARDOZA'S POKER NEWSLETTER
www.cardozapub.com
An upcoming poker newsletter by my publisher, Avery Cardoza, the world's foremost publisher of poker and gambling books.

LIST OF PLACES TO DISCUSS POKER

Ever wanted to discuss a poker idea with a colleague or get advice from an expert? Have you ever had the notion to share a new poker idea or express an opinion? Want to know the latest news and gossip about poker? Or, maybe, like me, you usually just want to sit back and find out what others are saying about poker.

The Internet is filled with places where you can do just that. I'm not talking about voice conversations or even live conversations, such as you might find in a chat room. Rather I'm talking about bulletin board type discussions where you type anything from a one-word retort to a long, thoughtful article on your computer, then—with a single click—upload it to a remote computer that is accessible to everyone, so the whole world can see your new discussion topic or your reply to someone else's.

Until the Internet came along, these things were hard to do. You had to find the right people in the right places in the right moods. Otherwise, poker didn't get discussed, except face-to-face among the few of us who lived the game daily.

And, looking back, it's amazing to remember how little we knew about the broad poker world. Newspapers didn't cover poker much, and there were no publications devoted to the game. You had to get your news through the grapevine, and it was incomplete.

But the world has changed and I'm sure that a few years down the road, we'll look back on what's happening online today and consider it primitive.

If you want to stay on top of poker today, you might try some of the discussion forums shown below. I visit from time to time, and doing so is a good idea if you take poker seriously enough and want to stay up-to-date.

CARO AND BRUNSON FORUM
www.poker1.com

This forum invites polite conversation about poker. It is endorsed by Doylesroom.com and Mike Caro University of Poker (MCU). Both Mike and I participate in the conversations.

REC.GAMBLING.POKER

Use newsreader to access **rec.gambling.poker**. Also, you can access RGP through www.google.com by searching the newsgroups.

There's good discussion and information here, but you have to sift through hundreds of juvenile outbusts, off-topic ranting, lies, libel, and vulgarity to get anything out of it. I guess that's the nature of an unmoderated public forum where unhappy people can post anonymously just to get attention. But, despite our high hopes for RGP, many of us in the public eye have stopped posting there, because we tend to be targets and it isn't any longer a comfortable place to exchange ideas. On the other hand, most posts *are* polite and many are informative. If you can tolerate the occasionally rude and anonymous falsehood and gossip, you'll find value here.

TWO PLUS TWO FORUM
www.twoplustwo.com

This informative forum, affiliated with a poker publisher, occasionally seems partial to the arguments of its primary authors—Mason Malmuth and David Sklansky—at the expense of other authorities. Still an excellent site to visit and learn.

THE BENEFITS OF ONLINE LEARNING

You can use discussion sites for learning poker by asking more experienced players questions or you can share your own expertise. These sites are also a good place to discuss poker personalities, tournaments, rules, and the poker lifestyle. Enter with a thick skin, though. Since other people can post anonymously, a small, boisterous minority—seemingly without quality lives of their own to lead—often try to disrupt the forums by posting insults, slander, outrageous falsehoods, and vulgarity. I've learned through experience that these posters are better ignored than reasoned with. If you respond to them, you just provide them with the attention they're craving and reinforce their repugnant behavior.

The poker online experience will improve. Many new sites will come along, so keep your eyes open. And, remember, the Internet is in transition. The lessons will be more automated and useful. And, hopefully, even the discussions will become more civil and meaningful. Yeah, right! Human nature never changes, so online, as in the real world, you'll always encounter misfits. When you do, just remember that their character is already in question. But how you deal with them and the situations you journey through in poker and in life speak to *your* character.

As you begin or continue your online poker journey, please treat our great game with the respect it deserves.

♠ ♥ ♦ ♣

Getting Started Online

Before you can play, you need to go to your desired online poker site and download the software onto your computer. Once this is done, you'll need to install the program on your machine, which, as you'll see, is easy. I'm going to take you through this process as it would be done in doylesroom.com.

You'll forgive me for using Doyle's Room as an example, but it's the one I'm most familiar with. Other sites have very similar procedures.

HOW TO DOWNLOAD THE SOFTWARE

STEP 1. GO TO THE HOME PAGE

Open your browser, type www.doylesroom.com in the address bar, and click the "Go" button or hit Enter on your keyboard.

You'll land here…

STEP 2. BEGIN THE DOWNLOAD

Click the big blue button near the bottom that's labeled, "Download Now—Click Here!" You'll come to a new page with the same button toward the top, surrounded by some information you may want to read. Click that button again.

STEP 3. BEGIN THE DOWNLOAD

A box will pop up on your screen that looks like this...

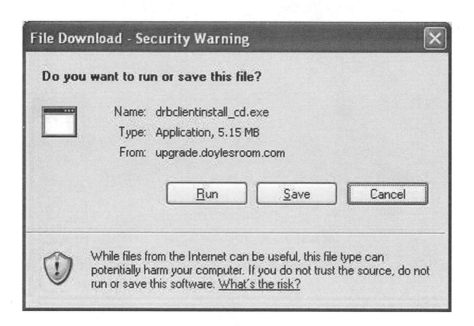

You can either click RUN (which is a quicker download) or SAVE—as it puts the installation program right on your hard drive, which is recommended. In this example, we're going to choose SAVE. Soon, you'll run that program and it will automatically install the poker-playing software.

You'll now see another box and have an opportunity to choose a folder on your computer to place the downloaded install program. Remember the name of the folder you choose. In this case, we've chosen a folder called "Downloaded." You probably won't have a folder with that name, unless you created one. And the list of your folders won't look like those shown on this machine. It will look like whatever folders you have on *your* machine. Whatever the case, it's important to remember the folder name you choose in the "Save in:" field at the top of the box. If you don't like the folder suggested, you can use the dropdown arrow (V) to the right of the "Save in:" field to choose a different one.

The box on your screen will look similar to this...

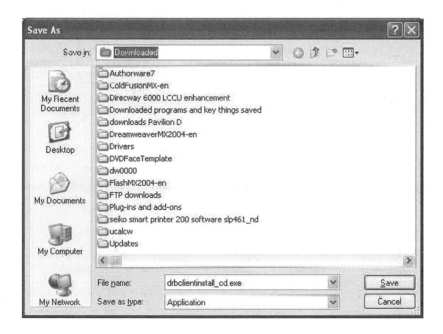

Now, click the SAVE button. Depending on the speed of your connection, dial-up or broadband, the download can take as little as a minute or up to 15 minutes or longer.

Once this is done, you're ready for Step 4, the easiest of all. Your first experience with online play is only minutes away, and if it strikes you the way it struck me the first time, the experience is going to be thrilling. Who could have imagined poker like this twenty years ago?

It's time to take the final step.

STEP 4. DO THE FINAL INSTALL

You have the software, so it's time to install it. Now, unless you decided to run the installation directly rather than save it, just find the file in the folder you chose and double click on it. You'll be walked through the installation and sign-up process and be playing in minutes!

Anytime you want to play poker in the future, just click on the Doyle's Room icon…

THE SOFTWARE

You might expect to play online without installing software on your own machine—by playing directly on the web—but that isn't usually how it works: The games function more reliably if each player has the same software loaded on a personal computer. Binding all these personal computers together is another computer, perhaps halfway around the globe, that sends required data and messages from each player to the others. This controlling computer is called a "server." Think of it as a faraway dealer that shuffles, distributes cards to each player around the world, makes sure players act in turn, decides who wins, and awards the pots. It also allows the exchange of open table chat that everyone can see.

NOTE ON MACS

Unfortunately, if you're looking for software that runs on a Macintosh or other personal computer other than the ubiquitous PC running Windows, you're probably out of luck. Most software is only developed for Microsoft Windows at this time. The good news, they tell me, is that Mac users can often add Windows compatibility software to their computers and join the worldwide online poker explosion.

♠♥♦♣

Playing for Free
or for
Real-Money

Most sites, including Doyle's Room, allow you to practice for free. But since what's involved has no real value, other than bragging rights, you'll probably find the free games full of players who don't care how much they lose on a pot—as long as they have some chance of winning.

This means, free-game players tend to be very loose, often unrealistically so. You see, there's something about real money that makes players more sensible about the hands they play and how they play them. When there's absolutely no money at stake, many players seem to participate in almost every pot, no matter how bad the decision to play a hand or call a bet seems to be. The reason, I guess, is that there's no penalty for losing. If you want to get a better sense of how opponents play when they have something at stake, you'll have to investigate the real-money games.

GET A TASTE BY PLAYING SMALL MONEY GAMES

Remember, that you don't need to play for big money or even any money at all. But if you tire of the free games, you can try limits as small as two cent and four cent— meaning all the early bets and raises are by increments of two cents and later they become four cents. Almost anyone can afford that and still experience the thrill of playing poker for actual money.

Now, you wouldn't think that just making the bets a couple of cents would make much difference. I didn't. But now I realize that the number of players who enter a pot and the quality of their decisions is remarkably better, even if the battle is only over a few cents per bet.

Spreading tiny real-money games is a service that online poker rooms can offer to the world, whereas real-world casinos couldn't do the same thing profitably. Those real casinos have dealers to pay, physical facilities to maintain, and much more. They just couldn't earn enough by extracting a penny or two from each pot in tra-ditional rakes to get anywhere close to breaking even.

These are tremendous break-in games for new play-ers. You get the taste of real-money play. And even if you lose, the cost of entertainment is trivial compared to even going to a movie or dinner. For this small cost, you're beginning your poker education through live play. I wish this opportunity had been available when I first began to think about poker and to actually play it.

I'm not saying that you need to play for real-money at all. It's up to you. However, you can take an important first step into poker by playing in the free poker games offered by most major sites. If you do so, you'll risk nothing and you'll quickly master the mechanics of the games, learn the rules, and become able to understand the strengths and weaknesses of common hands. Some players choose to play in the free games indefinitely. Others move on to the cash games.

PLAYING BIGGER MONEY GAMES

If you play for money, I advise you to gradually move up your betting limits. Poker isn't going to be fun if you risk more money than you're comfortable risking. This is especially true at first when so much of your thought process will be taken up by mastering the software. Even though the software is easy to operate, make sure you know the ins and outs before risking money that's important to you. I hope you—and all others exploring online poker for the first time—heed that advice.

FUNDING YOUR ACCOUNT
GETTING MONEY INTO THE GAME

If you choose to play for real money, you need to get money to your desired online poker site so you have a bankroll there. This is fairly simple: All you have to do is follow the onscreen instructions after visiting the site.

You'll be given a choice of sending money by check or wire, providing credit card information, or using a service such as NETeller. Most players find that the use of NETeller is the easiest and quickest way to fund their online poker account, which is why this service is the preferred method for many major sites, including Doyle's Room. Note that some sites will even give you an extra bonus for using NETeller. You can learn more about that service by visiting www.neteller.com.

I'm not going to tax your mind here by going through the whole process of getting funds into your poker account, but you'll find you can quickly be playing for real money just by following the onscreen instructions. In any case, whichever method you decide to use, the poker site you choose will guide you through the choices and the easiest way to go about depositing funds so you can begin playing even if the site resides in a different country than your own.

Keep in mind that if you send a check or wire funds, it's going to take a while before you can use the chips you've purchased in actual games. And, if you use a credit card directly, you might find it difficult to purchase chips at all. Depending on the card you hold, the credit issuer may decline the use of your card for this purpose.

Also, most sites offer a valuable bonus for signing up, and Doyle's Room is no exception. That is like free extra money to get you started.

CASHING OUT OF A GAME

When you'd like to cash out some or all of the money in your account, it's as easy as visiting the cashier and making a request. Again, all you need to do is follow the online instructions. I recommend you try this soon after you join so you can get comfortable with this process. Just ask for a cash out of a few dollars to satisfy your curiosity to see how the system works.

While the procedure to add money to your account is easy, it's not quite as easy as just taking money out of your pocket at a real-world casino and buying as many chips as you want. So naturally, I don't recommend that you cash out often, unless you have sufficient funds to cover a bad run of hands.

So, be sensible and keep money in your account. It's more cumbersome to replenish your funds online.

Finally, before we move on, I want to remind you that you absolutely *don't* have to play for real money at all.

The Basic Rules and Procedures of Play

I realize that some of you may be brand new to poker—and we all were in the beginning—and you will be using the Internet as your first regular poker experience. So to help you along the way, this section will present a few basics.

These rules and procedures apply to poker on the Internet and in traditional real-world games, except where noted.

A FEW BASICS
THE DECK OF CARDS

The deck is made up of 52 cards, consisting of 13 ranks. They are, from highest to lowest, ace (A), king (K), queen (Q), jack (J), 10, 9, 8, 7, 6, 5, 4, 3 (sometimes called "trey"), and 2 (usually called "deuce"). There are four instances of each rank in the deck, one for each of four suits: clubs, diamonds, hearts, and spades. The suits are all of equal value.

BASIC HAND RANKINGS

In the common forms of poker, you're always selecting your best five cards. Here's how they rank, borrowed with permission from the book *Fundamental Secrets of Winning Poker (Mike Caro), Cardoza Publishing*—as are the subsequent game descriptions, which I've modified for online poker play.

FIVE-CARD POKER HAND VALUES

(Applicable to almost all poker games where high hand wins)

Hands are listed in descending order from the strongest, the royal flush, to the weakest, no pair hands.

ROYAL FLUSH *Example:* A♣ K♣ Q♣ J♣ 10♣
Described: Five cards of consecutive ranks from ace down to ten, all the same suit. (Royal flush is merely the best straight flush.)
Ties: Two or more royal flushes divide the pot.

STRAIGHT FLUSH *Example:* 9♦ 8♦ 7♦ 6♦ 5♦
Described: Five cards of consecutive ranks, all the same suit. (Ace can be used low to form a five-high straight flush.)
Ties: Higher ranking straight wins. If tied, the pot is split.

FOUR OF A KIND *Example:* 3♣ 3♦ 3♥ 3♠ K♣
Described: Four cards of a matching rank, plus an extra card.
Ties: Highest ranking four of a kind wins. If tied, higher extra card wins.

FULL HOUSE *Example:* 9♣ 9♥ 9♠ Q♦ Q♠
Described: Three cards of matching rank, plus two cards of a different matching rank.
Ties: Higher rank of the three of a kind within the full house wins.

FLUSH *Example:* A♠ J♠ 7♠ 6♠ 2♠
Described: Five cards of the same suit that do not qualify as a straight flush or royal flush.
Ties: Highest ranking card wins. If those are the same, next highest card wins, and so forth.

STRAIGHT *Example:* 8♦ 7♠ 6♦ 5♣ 4♥
Described: Five ranks in sequence. (Ace can be used low to form a five-high straight.)
Ties: Higher rank beginning the sequence wins.

THREE OF A KIND *Example:* A♦ A♣ A♥ Q♦ 4♠
Described: Three cards of a matching rank and two extra cards whose ranks do not match.
Ties: Higher rank of the three of a kind wins. If tied, higher extra card wins.

TWO PAIR *Example:* K♥ K♦ 4♥ 4♠ A♠
Described: Two cards of a matching rank, plus two cards of another matching rank, plus one extra card.
Ties: Highest pair wins. If tied, higher second pair wins. If still tied, higher extra card wins.

ONE PAIR *Example:* 7♠ 7♥ Q♥ 10♠ 3♣
Described: Two cards of a matching rank, plus three extra cards of all different ranks.
Ties: Higher pair wins. If ranks are the same, highest ranking extra card *not matched by opponent* wins.

NO PAIR *Example:* Q♠ J♥ 8♥ 6♦ 2♠
Described: Any hand that does not qualify for one of the categories listed above.
Ties: Highest card wins. If the hands tie for high card, the second highest cards are compared, and so forth.

The order in which your poker cards are arranged doesn't matter. Therefore, 9♥ 10♦ Q♦ 8♣ J♠ is exactly the same as Q♦ J♠ 10♦ 9♥ 8♣. It makes no difference whether you go to the trouble of sorting your cards or not; you still have a straight.

The ace is not always the highest rank. Sometimes it can be used as the smallest card in this straight or straight flush: 5-4-3-2-A. Five-high is the *worst* straight or straight flush you can get, and it doesn't beat 6-5-4-3-2, even though it contains an ace. In this case, you should think of an ace as a "1," lower than a "2." An ace has the versatility to be used as a "1" when it completes a five-high sequence. Otherwise it is the highest rank—above a king.

HOW HOLD'EM IS PLAYED

When people first learn hold'em, they're surprised to learn that your secret hand consists of just two cards. At first that seems like a pitifully few number of cards for a sophisticated poker game. But pretty quickly they realize just how deceptive this game is. Two cards—the only ones that are private to you and that nobody else sees—is plenty. When they interact in sometimes complex and unexpected ways with the five "community" cards dealt face up that belong to everyone, all sorts of fireworks can happen.

Online, hold'em is far and away more common than seven-stud, although stud remains in second place, followed by Omaha high-low split, a relative newcomer to poker that beginners should probably avoid until they have mastered hold'em and stud. At the time I write this, Doyle's Room specializes in hold'em games, with Omaha and Omaha high-low games also offered. We'll soon add seven-card stud and a few other popular poker forms—and these might already be available as you read these words.

THE NEW ERA OF HOLD'EM

In the traditional world of poker outside the Internet, hold'em hasn't been the dominant game until recently, in 2003, though it *has been* the world championship game, since way back when the World Series of Poker began in the early seventies. I was appalled to realize that until just a few years ago, even the rules of hold'em weren't commonly known, except in those Southern regions and Texas, where I'd developed my poker skills long ago—and in public casinos.

Before the recent wave of televised world class poker tournaments and the advent of Internet poker, the beauty of *my* game—hold'em—didn't directly translate into popularity in games throughout many regions of the United States and elsewhere in the world. Now, hold'em is everywhere. It's far and away the most common form of poker played online.

In the years ahead, you might see other forms of poker take hold on the Internet. Maybe brand new types of poker will be invented and become popular. But I'm betting my money that hold'em will be the staple game for many years to come. It's captured the heart and soul of players throughout the world.

LIMIT, NO-LIMIT AND POT-LIMIT HOLD'EM

Most online casinos offer hold'em in at least two versions: limit and no limit. In **limit**, the exact size of every bet or raise you make is determined in advance. In the later betting rounds, it's always twice as much as it is on the early betting rounds. In **no-limit**, you can bet in an almost unlimited range, starting with a minimum bet that's equal to the size of the big blind, which is a required bet that the player two seats to the left of the dealer position makes, to as many chips as you have on the table.

Another method of betting is called **pot limit**. This is kind of an intermediate battleground bridging limit and no limit games. In pot-limit games, you can't always bet all the chips you have in front of you; you're limited by the size of the pot. But the pot can grow quickly as bets, raises, and calls occur, and huge money can change hands on a single showdown.

The maximum number of opponents who sit in a hold'em game is usually limited to ten, but more commonly only nine chairs are put at a table.

LIMIT HOLD'EM

The following modified description of how to play hold'em is borrowed from *Cardoza Publishing* and first appeared in the book *Fundamental Secrets of Winning Poker (Mike Caro)*. All rules and procedures have been modified to conform to online poker.

We're going to use a $4/$8 game as an example to show how limit hold'em is played. A $4/$8 game means that all bets and raises in the first two betting rounds will be for $4, and in the last two rounds, for $8. Since the bets are regulated, this game would be known as limit poker.

But don't be fooled by the word "limit." Some of the biggest hold'em games played are limit games and involve sessions where more than $500,000 can be won or lost.

22 IS WRONG—23 IS RIGHT!

You might have heard that 22 is the maximum theoretical number of players that can sit at a hold'em table. The math is based on a 52 card deck, two cards to each player, making a total of 44 used up for starting hands. That leaves eight cards in the deck. Now, five of those will comprise the board—the five cards that will be turned face-up by the dealer to be shared by everyone. The final three are used for the "burn"—a procedure that the dealer uses to waste one card before dealing the flop, the turn, and the river (which you'll soon learn about). The purpose of burn cards is to make doubly sure that no one can identify the next card that will be dealt after a betting round—usually because it was inadvertently exposed on top of the deck.

But 22 is the wrong maximum number of players online where burning doesn't make any sense. Since there's no physical deck online, and no risk of exposed cards, there are three extra cards that come into play, and you could use two of them to add one more player. Now, the reason for me saying this isn't trivial. I fully expect to see 23-handed games come online somewhere—just as a novelty. Perhaps, they'll even gain popularity. Imagine the huge pots that would be possible!

LIMIT HOLD'EM RULES AND PROCEDURES

1. The first two players to the left of the dealer **button**— which marks the position of where an actual player-dealer would be if participants took turns dealing—are required to post the blinds. A **blind bet** is a wager a player is required to put in the pot before receiving any cards. In our example game, the player immediately to the left of the dealer puts in a blind bet of $2 and the player two seats to the left of the dealer puts in $4. In online sites, this is all handled automatically by the software. So, in this game, there is $6 in the pot that players that can compete for even before any cards are dealt. (Note: There is usually no ante in hold'em.)

2. The computer shuffles and distributes one card at a time face down to each player, beginning to the left of the button, and continuing clockwise until each participant has two cards. These two cards are the only ones each player will receive during a hand of hold'em.

3. The action begins with the player to the left of the big blind. Each player, acting clockwise in turn, must call the previous bet, raise it $4, or throw the hand away.

4. All bets are added to the pot, along with the original blinds, in the center of the table.

5. If you bet or raise and all your opponents fold, you win what's in the pot, and there is no subsequent dealing or betting on this hand.

6. If there are callers and no raise, the big blind has the option to "raise," even though he has only been called. This is called a **live blind**.

7. If two or more players remain after the first round of betting, the deal continues. Three face-up cards will be dealt all at once in the center of the table. This is called the **flop**.

8. Players coordinate the two secret cards held in their hand with the three cards face up on the board to form their five-card poker hand. There is a second round of betting, beginning to the left of the dealer. All bets remain at the pre-established $4 limits.

9. If two or more players remain after the second round of betting, the deal continues. The dealer turns over a fourth communal board card in the center of the table. This is called the **turn** card.

10. There is a third round of betting, beginning with the first active player to the left of the dealer. All bets now double to $8.

11. If two or more players remain after the third round of betting, the deal continues. The dealer delivers a fifth and final communal board card in the center of the table. It's called the **river** card.

12. There is a fourth and final round of betting, beginning to the left of the dealer. All bets remain at $8.

13. If two or more players remain after the final betting round, there is a **showdown** to determine the winner. The computer turns the winning two cards face up on the table. The best hand is determined by incorporating those two cards and any of the five communal board cards to form the best traditional five-card poker hand. The player having that best hand wins all the money in the pot.

14. The dealer button moves clockwise, one spot to the left, the blind bets are placed for the next hand, and the process is repeated.

NO-LIMIT HOLD'EM RULES AND PROCEDURES

The above description for playing limit hold'em is identical to how no-limit hold'em is played with just one exception: the amount that can be bet. The minimum starting bet must be at least the size of the big blind, while the maximum allowed can be any amount up to the number of chips you hold. For example, if you're playing heads up, your opponent has bet $4, and you have $92 in front of you, you can push in all those chips—go **all-in**. In limit poker, your raise would be restricted to just $4.

In a real-world game, when you want to make a bet, you push your chips out in front of you. When you want to fold, you toss your cards away. But when playing online, where there are no physical elements of the game to interact with—just a computer screen and keyboard—the only way to act on a hand is to click on a button.

Let's take a look and see how this works online.

HOW TO BET NO-LIMIT HOLD'EM ONLINE

We'll step into Doyle's Room to see what the betting choices might look like online in a no-limit hold'em game.

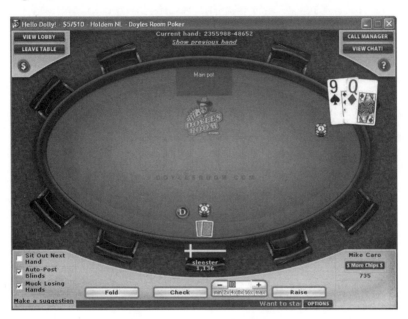

Here, you're in the big blind and have just been called. Because there's a "live blind," you are allowed to raise. You have an opportunity to decide how much to wager. If it weren't for the live blind rule, the action would be over and we'd be looking at the flop.

In addition to clicking Fold or Check, you can click Raise. What happens if you do? Well, you'll end up raising the amount that's written in the white area between the minus sign and the plus sign. In Doyle's Room, the amount shown defaults to the size of the previous bet, so if you just click raise without changing it, you'll always be doubling the last wager. In this case, the "last bet" was the big blind, $10.

Look closely, and you'll see that you have many other options. Click minimum (Min) and the raise stays the same, because the smallest legal raise is always the size of the bet, assuming both players have enough chips to cover it. The "Min" button is more useful when you're first to act on subsequent betting rounds. Click maximum (Max) and you're wagering all the chips in front of you, going all-in.

Then there are smaller buttons below, marked "2x," "4x," "8x," and "16x." Those do exactly what you'd expect. Click 4x and your pending bet is changed to four times $10 or $40. But you don't actually place this wager until you press the Raise (or Bet) button.

You can also make odd bets online, typing in any amount you wish to wager. For instance, you can type in $73 or $117 for a bet or raise, though typing in these unusual amounts—as apposed to just clicking a button—just slows down the game.

HOW TO READ HOLD'EM HANDS

In hold'em, your final hand is formed from a combination of the two cards you hold in private with the five community cards available to both you and your opponents. Whatever the best five cards are, that's your hand. In order to form the best hand possible, both private cards may be used, just one of them, or none at all. If none are used, the five communal cards—the **board**—is played and the best a player can hope for is a tie.

For example, the five-card community board is:

Your Hand   **Your Opponent**

You have the best hand by using just one card, your 10, to make a K-Q-J-10-9 straight. Your opponent has K-K-K-A-Q, three kings, but despite it's powerful looks, it isn't good enough.

In the following example, you split the pot.

The board is…

Your Hand   **Your Opponent**

Up until that last card, your hand was aces up (aces over eights) and your opponent was hoping to make a spade flush. He missed the flush, but suddenly the hand on the board is aces over kings with a nine kicker. Neither of your two cards come into play, because they can't improve what's on the board. The same is true for your opponent. So, you split the pot, without either of you using a card in your hand.

HOW SEVEN-CARD STUD IS PLAYED

Up until a few years ago, seven-card stud was probably the most played form of poker in the United States, in both casinos and home games. Hold'em has recently claimed that territory, especially on the Internet. But stud is still popular, and—who knows—it might be ready to challenge hold'em again in the future. You just never know with gamblers. I've lived though a lot of changes surrounding poker. And few things could surprise me.

In any case, seven-card stud is a game you should know. Here's how you play it...

OVERVIEW

The maximum number of players at a table is usually seven, though you'll sometimes see eight. Eight-handed play can be awkward in loose games, because if everyone stays in, there won't be enough cards to play out the hands.

Some of your cards are dealt face down for only you to look at, while others are dealt face up to be examined by everyone. In all, if the hand doesn't terminate prematurely because a bet is uncalled, seven cards will be dealt to the players—three face down and four face up.

We'll use a $5/$10 game as an example to see how the game works.

SEVEN-CARD STUD RULES AND PROCEDURES

1. All players at your table **ante** by placing a mandatory token bet before receiving any cards. In our example game with $5 and $10 limits, each player antes $1.

2. The computer shuffles and distributes one card at a time face down to each player, beginning to the left of the dealer button—which marks the position of where an actual player-dealer would be if participants took turns dealing—continuing clockwise, until each participant has three cards. The first two cards dealt to each player are face down and are looked at only by the player holding those cards; the third is face up.

3. The lowest-ranking card among those dealt face up—known as **door cards**—is forced to make a token starting bet of $2. This is called the **bring in** bet. Note that the size of the bring-in will depend on how large or how small a limit you choose. If two or more cards tie for lowest rank, the "low" suit determines the player that must make the bet. Even though no suit is worth more than another in poker, for this purpose, the lowest rank is clubs, followed by diamonds, hearts, and then spades (alphabetical order, lowest suit first).

4. Beginning with the player to the left of the $2 starting bet, each player must either *complete* the previous bet, bringing it up to the first $5 level, raise it $5 if the bet is already at $5, or throw the hand away.

5. All bets are added to the pot, along with the original antes, in the center of the table.

6. If you bet or raise and all your opponents fold, you win what's in the pot, and there is no subsequent dealing or betting.

7. If two or more players remain after the first round of betting, the deal continues. The computer-dealer delivers a fourth card, face up, to each remaining player in turn, beginning at his left.

8. There is a second round of betting, beginning with the player who has the highest-ranking exposed pair (face up) on board, or if there is no pair, then the highest-ranking exposed card. If two players have high cards of equal rank, the higher-ranking second face-up card determines who acts first. If *both* cards rank the same, the player nearest to the dealer button's left acts first. All bets remain at the pre-established $5 limits, unless a player has an exposed pair on board, where he has the option to bet $10.

9. If two or more players remain after the second round of betting, the deal continues. The dealer delivers a fifth card, face up, to each remaining player in turn, beginning at his left.

10. There is a third round of betting, beginning with the player who has the highest-ranking exposed (face up) hand. If two players have equally high pairs, or high cards of equal rank, the higher-ranking face-up odd card determines who acts first. All bets now double to $10.

11. If two or more players remain after the third round of betting, the deal continues. The dealer delivers a sixth card, face up, to each remaining player in turn, beginning at the dealer's left.

12. There is a fourth round of betting, beginning with the player who has the highest-ranking exposed hand, according to the same criteria as before. All bets remain at $10.

13. If two or more players remain after the fourth round of betting, the deal continues. The dealer delivers a seventh and final card, face down, to each remaining player in turn, beginning at the dealer's left.

14. There is a fifth and final round of betting, beginning with the player who has the highest-ranking exposed hand. All bets remain at $10.

15. If two or more players remain after the final betting round, there is a showdown to determine the winner. The computer turns the best five-card hand face up on the table, and the holder of that hand wins all the money in the pot.

16. Everyone antes for the next hand, and the process is repeated.

HOW OTHER FORMS OF ONLINE POKER ARE PLAYED

There are three other forms of poker for which I'd like to provide the rules: Omaha, Omaha high-low split, and old-fashioned five-card draw poker. The two types of Omaha are pretty common online. Doyle's Room already offers them. Draw poker is harder to find, but I'm including rules for it, because it's the fountainhead game that marks the early stages of poker's tradition. And I'm guessing it will always have a small, but loyal, following.

So you understand the distinctions between the different Omaha variations, **Omaha** or **Omaha High** is the form of the game played for high only. **Omaha High-Low Split** or **Omaha High-Low Eight-or-Better** is the form of the game where the best high hand splits the pot with the best low hand, as long as the low hand has five unmatched cards that are 8 or below. If no player holds an eight-or-better low hand, than the high hand wins the entire pot.

OMAHA RULES AND PROCEDURES

1. The blind structure is exactly the same as in hold'em.

2. The computer shuffles and distributes one card at a time face down to each player, beginning to the left of the dealer button—which marks the position of where an actual player-dealer would be if participants took turns dealing—continuing clockwise, until each participant has four cards. These four cards are the only ones each player will receive during a hand of Omaha.

3. The number of betting rounds and the predefined amount of bets on each round are exactly the same as for a hold'em game of the same size.

4. If two or more players remain after the final betting round, there is a showdown to determine the winner. The computer turns the winning four cards face up on the table. The best hand is determined

by incorporating *exactly* two of the privately held cards and *exactly* three of the five communal board cards to form the best traditional five-card poker hand. The player having that best hand wins all the money in the pot.

5. The blind bets are placed for the next hand, and the process is repeated.

HOW TO READ OMAHA HANDS

In Omaha, in order to form the best hand possible, both private cards must be used. Unlike in hold'em, you cannot play just one of your cards or play what's on the board, hoping for a tie. Also, you can't use three or four of your private cards—only two, and *exactly* two.

Let's look at an example:

The Board:

Your Hand:

Your Opponent:

  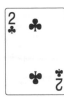

You lose! This isn't immediately intuitive to all players who sample Omaha for the first time. Your opponent's hand looks pathetic compared to yours. But, remember, you must use *exactly* two cards from your hand. Which ones? The best you can come up with is a full house, kings over deuces, by playing the K-2. It seems like those aces should factor in there somewhere, because they're so pretty. But, they don't. You can't play the pair of aces, because using those two cards would only give you A-A-K-K-J.

You're opponent gets to play K-J for his full house, and, sadly, kings-full over jacks is better than kings-full over deuces.

Likewise, it's easy for beginners to think they have a full house in Omaha, when there isn't one there. Take a look at this hand, for instance…

The Board:

Your Hand:

You can only use the two tens to make three of a kind. You can't play a pair of jacks or queens in addition to that. Look at this hand:

The Board:

Your Hand:

It's natural to suppose you hold something monstrous if it's your first night at the Omaha table. Is there a royal flush? No, because you can only use two of those three clubs. And stop looking, you don't have even a pair.

Omaha can be so deceptive at first that I recommend you only play it for small stakes until you get acclimated. Or play it just for fun online.

OMAHA HIGH-LOW EIGHT-OR-BETTER RULES AND PROCEDURES

All rules and procedures are exactly the same as for Omaha, except:

1. The pot is divided into two halves. One half will be awarded to the best high hand; one half will be awarded to the best low hand.

2. A player *can*, but doesn't need to, use the same two cards to make both a best low hand and a best high hand.

3. You need at least an 8 to qualify for the low half of the pot. If nobody qualifies for the low half by holding an 8 or better, the highest hand wins the whole pot. Note that whenever Omaha high-low split is played, it is *usually*—in fact, these days almost exclusively—with the eight-or-better to qualify for the low end of the pot.

4. After both the high and low halves of the pot are awarded, the computer-dealer shuffles again, and the process is repeated.

HOW TO DETERMINE THE BEST LOW HAND IN OMAHA HIGH-LOW SPLIT

The best low hand possible in Omaha high-low split is 5-4-3-2-A. For the purpose of determining a low hand, straights and flushes are ignored, so they don't count against a hand, and an ace is always considered lower, or better, than a deuce, with king being the highest, or worst rank.

Any five-card hand without a pair always beats a hand with a pair. If two or more hands contain a pair, the winning hand is the one that *loses* if traditional high-hand values were used to determine a winner, with the exception of aces being the lowest pair.

The lowest-ranking *high* card in a five-card hand determines the winner among unpaired hands. If those high cards are of the same rank between competing hands, the second highest ranks are compared, then the third, and so on, until the winner is determined.

We'll take a look at four examples so you fully understand how the low hand is determined in Omaha high-low eight-or-better.

1. In this example, the first hand beats the second hand for low, because the first hand has no pair and flushes don't count against a low hand.

Winning Low Hand:

Losing Low Hand:

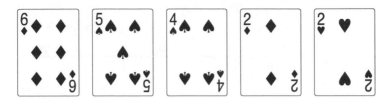

2. Here, the 7-high hand beats the 8-high hand—note that the ace is considered low in the 7-high hand.

Winning Low Hand:

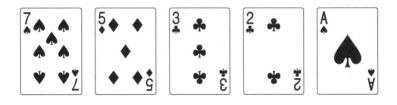

Losing Low Hand:

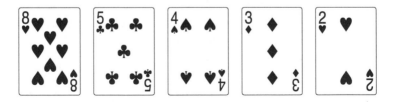

3. In the following example, the first hand wins because the lowest-ranking high card is a 9, versus a jack in the second hand, and straights don't count against a low hand.

Winning Low Hand:

Losing Low Hand:

4. Here is a rare example of a pair of kings winning the low end of the pot, for a simple reason: One pair of kings is lower than two pair!

Winning Low Hand:

Losing Low Hand:

HOW TO DETERMINE THE BEST HIGH-LOW HAND IN OMAHA HIGH-LOW SPLIT

As I said earlier, you can use the same two cards to make both a best low hand and a best high hand, or you can use a different two-card combination from your hand. Following are two examples to make this clear.

The Board:

Your Hand:

Your best high hand is three eights with a queen and a 7, using the 8-8 from your hand, and your best low hand is unbeatable—but might be tied—7-4-3-2-A, using the A-2 from your hand.

In following example, you use the same two cards for high and low.

The Board:

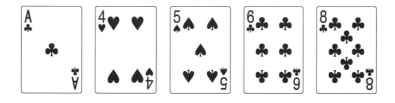

Your Hand

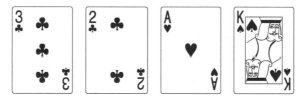

Here you use the 3-2 of clubs to make the best possible low hand, 5-4-3-2-A, and at the same time make the club flush for high, A-8-6-3-2.

FIVE-CARD DRAW RULES AND PROCEDURES

Because it's so easy to run out of cards, the maximum number of participants in a draw poker game usually is limited to eight.

Most people have seen five-card draw played in the movies and already have some idea about how it's played. All the cards you're dealt arrive facedown. There are no exposed cards in draw poker until the showdown. You wager on those original five cards. Then, if there are still two or more players contesting the pot, you draw cards, exchanging those you don't like for ones you hope you'll like better. Then you bet again. If the pot is still contested, meaning it wasn't surrendered without a fight, there's a showdown to determine the winner. Online, remember, the computer does this for you. The winning hand will always be determined correctly when shown down.

These procedures for draw assume a $5/$10 betting limit.

1. All players at your table ante by placing a mandatory token bet before receiving any cards. In our example game with $5/$10 limits, each player antes $1.

2. The computer shuffles.

3. The computer-dealer distributes one card at a time face down to each player, beginning to the left of the dealer button and continuing clockwise. The deal continues until each player has five cards.

4. There is an initial round of betting. Beginning to the left of the dealer, each player looks at his hand and decides what to do. In old-fashioned "guts-to-open" poker, there are no minimum requirements to make the initial bet of $5, also known as **opening the pot**, so you can bet on raw courage if you want to. But if you're playing the popular variation called **jacks-or-better**, you need a least a pair of jacks to open for $5.

5. If the pot has already been opened by someone else when the action reaches you, you may fold, call the $5, or raise $5, making it a total of $10. If the pot has not already been opened, you can bet or check. If you're the last person to act and nobody has opened, you can also check, and the hand will end without a winner. Then the next hand is dealt.

6. If there is betting, all antes and bets will be added to the pot.

7. If you bet or raise and all your opponents fold, you win what's in the pot, and there is no subsequent draw or betting.

8. If two or more players remain after the first round of betting, each remaining player, in turn—beginning at the dealer's left—can take replacements in an attempt to improve a hand. You may discard from one to all five unwanted cards and immediately be dealt new ones. Or you can **stand pat**—meaning you're satisfied with the cards you already have and don't want any cards exchanged.

9. There is a second and final round of betting, beginning with the player who opened the pot. All bets in this round are double the amount of the bets in the first round of betting—thus $10. If no one has bet when the action reaches you, you have the option of checking.

10. If you bet or raise and there is no call, the hand is over and you automatically win without a showdown.

11. If two or more players remain after the second and final betting round, there is a showdown to determine the winner. Cards are shown face up on the table, and the best hand wins all the money in the pot.

12. Everyone antes for the next hand, and the process is repeated.

Draw poker can be played with blinds, instead of, or in addition to antes. Also, some draw poker variations won't allow you to check before the draw. You'll have to either bet or throw your hand away. This is typically called a **pass and out** game.

Four Reasons Online Poker is Worse

Here are four ways that online poker is worse than real-world poker. I readily acknowledge that there are other minor grievances that could be added, but on reflection, these are the only four that impress me as being important.

REASON #1.
WHERE DID THE PHYSICAL TELLS GO?
The first thing you need to know is that you can throw your skills at reading opponents' body language out the window. In the very near future, I envision that you'll be able to see real opponents on your screen. Poker will

be like a video conference—and you'll be able to focus on the players across the table from you and read them. I predict, that live video of each player will replace the icons in the seats and tells will be everywhere. And then, full-scale psychological warfare will come to the online poker battlefield—and nothing will be missing.

ONLINE ICONS

But, for now, online poker sites—including DoylesRoom.com—depict players as icons. Sometimes those are cartoon characters, but Doyle's Room uses your choice of symbols, including flags, scenery, and artistic words, like "TILT."

Here are some of the icons you can choose to differentiate you at the tables from other players:

Think of it as selecting one of those weird pieces to represent you at Monopoly as you roll the dice and prance around the board. Players think it's kind of fun choosing their icon, but you're not going to gain any tells staring at them. Well, maybe that's not quite true. For instance, my guess is that players who choose an icon featuring the word "Tilt" are actually fairly tight players, trying to deceive you.

REASON #2.
CAN'T SPEND THE MONEY IMMEDIATELY

Part of the thrill of poker when I grew up is that you could send your opponents home with their tails tucked between their legs, whimpering and whining, while you're spending their freshly conquered money. Sadly, that thrill doesn't exist in online poker. You can't send opponents home whimpering, because they're *already* home whimpering. And you can't spend their money yet, because you can't physically touch it. It's there in your account, but if you want to spend it, you'll have to request a cash-out and it will be several days before it arrives.

Now, I'll wager you're thinking that might be a good thing. I'm sure there are thousands of poker players who unwisely wasted big chunks of their bankrolls after a big win who wish they'd had to wait a few days to receive their winnings.

DISCIPLINE NEEDED

It's hard for most players to acquire the discipline needed to hang on to a bankroll. And I think that playing online helps promote that necessary habit. But, I'm listing the fact that you can't spend the money immediately on the side of the scale that makes online poker worse, simply because I believe a grown-up poker player should be able to enjoy his winnings by stuffing them immediately into his pockets. Call me old fashioned, but anything else doesn't set quite right with me.

Except for that and the fact that you can't reach across the table and shake an opponents' hand or read him the way you can in a real game, online poker is just as good as the traditional kind we're accustomed to—and in some ways, it is better.

REASON #3.
YOU CAN'T GET MONEY INTO GAMES AS EASILY

You can't get money into games as easily online. I'd like to tell you that isn't the case, but I can't. You'll have to go through some gymnastics in order to fund an online account. In the real world, you can just walk into a casino, take money out of your pocket and begin playing!

If you're used to playing casino poker, you'll have to get accustomed to the process of putting chips on the table online. If you're playing just for fun, you won't have to go through this procedure right away. And, remember, I recommend that you *do* play just for fun until you feel comfortable with the software and think you're ready to risk cash. Some people may just want to play for fun for a long time, or even, for as long as they can go. That's fine, too. But, when you're ready to take the plunge, keep in mind that you can play for very small real-money stakes, just to test yourself. Many sites offer affordable stakes with $1 bets or less. You might even start at 10-cent wagers, which are offered at Doyle's Room.

The process for getting money online is similar at all online poker rooms. At DoylesRoom.com, for instance, you start the walk-through by simply going there, downloading the software, logging in, going to the cashier, and clicking "Set Up My Real Money Account," as seen below...

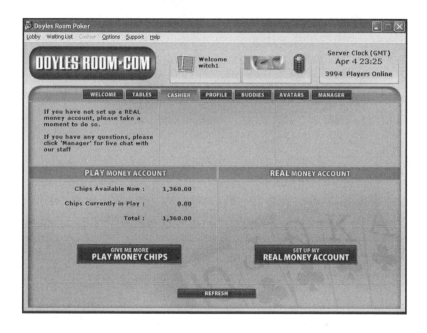

There is a compensating factor, however—you're not going to get robbed, a point I make in the following chapter.

REASON #4.
PARTNERSHIPS

Not being able to look your opponents in the eye and physically scrutinize them is certainly a disadvantage to online poker as compared to real-world games. In a live game, with your opponents sitting right in front of you, you can see who you're playing against, something that would be impossible to do against inanimate icons on your computer screen.

One of the main worries players have about online poker is that opponents may be playing partners. For example, what's to stop two opponents from getting on the phone and telling each other what cards they're holding? Then they can play their best hand or do other things that would be in their interest as a team. That's cheating, of course, and that runs contrary to the purpose of poker. But when money is involved, people sometimes will do things that are unethical.

People also worry about a single player pretending to be several opponents, using more than one computer and playing multiple hands from the same location. In real-world poker, obviously the problem of one person secretly playing a second hand is physically impossible, but, as in online games, collusion between partners working against you can still be a concern.

While it's difficult for partners to succeed online— good casino surveillance is able to pick up instances of collusion very quickly using tools I'll tell you about in the next chapter—some may still try. Just the same, you should still be alert for suspicious play and be ready to report instances to the site's management. In general, however, you're going to find online poker to be a safe environment to play.

Of course, I'm an advocate of ethical play. Poker is meant to be a selfish game. You need to play in your own best interest or the whole concept of fair competition breaks down.

Twenty-Four Reasons Online Poker is Better

I think every serious player prefers real-world poker at times. There's no substitute for being able to stare an opponent down and make decisions based on your observations. And there's no greater feeling in poker like that of intimidating opponents into making costly mistakes. Those elements are missing—and missed—when you play online.

Still, there are a great number of ways in which online poker actually excels. Each player has his own favorite reasons why he thinks online poker is in some way superior to real-world poker. These are mine...

REASON #1.
ALWAYS A GAME

Online poker makes a mockery out of how I went about finding good games when I traveled the poker circuit throughout Texas and the South in the 1960s and early 1970s. I mean, sometimes you'd drive all day only to find that the lucrative oil well you were hoping to drill had just dried up an hour before you got there. Then you had to swallow the disappointment and plan your next move in accordance with how much it would cost to travel. Was the game you'd heard about far down the road worth the hassle and the expense?

Then came casino poker. That helped, because there was often a choice of games in town. But many nights there was only one game of interest, and some nights there weren't any. So, imagine how I felt—having expended most of my effort finding the right games, rather than enjoying them—about being able to sit down at my computer on a sleepless night and find the best game in the world after a few mouse clicks.

What's even better is that poker never sleeps online. It's always prime time for poker somewhere in the world and you can join those games, even if nobody else is awake in your neighborhood.

REASON #2.
MEET OPPONENTS YOU'D
NEVER SEE IN PERSON

The Internet has made the world so much smaller. It might not look like it now, with all the political flare-ups and regional wars in the news, but I believe that encountering people from far away places and striking up instant friendships is bound to make life more civil eventually. You read about Internet romances that lead to marriage. And business associations are formed that would have been physically improbable before the Internet.

Bit by bit, poker is becoming the world's common language of gaming. In a real sense, online poker is doing its part to make the world better—as well as helping to showcase the game.

A main virtue of online poker is that it makes games possible among eager players who live so far apart that they'd seldom have a chance to sit down together at a real-world table.

REASON #3.
TAKE A QUICK
FIVE-MINUTE BREAK TO PLAY

If you had the urge to play poker prior to online play, with just a half-hour or less to spare, there wasn't anything you could do about it. That half-hour would be used up just getting near a casino. There certainly wouldn't be time to sit down and be dealt in. Now, that's all changed. Sometimes, I'll log into a game when I have just a few minutes to spare. I might only play half a dozen hands at $100/$200 limit, but so what? Usually, I wouldn't play that small, because—for me—it's not worth the effort. But those are hefty limits by online standards, where the target audience plays $15/$30 limits and often much smaller.

So, I play those few hands now, and I can do the same thing again on my next break—and those hands all add up, and so does the profit. It's a new aspect to poker I'd never considered possible until now.

REASON #4.
GREAT PRACTICE FOR THOSE NEW TO POKER

I'm betting one of the reasons that players haven't flocked to the poker rooms in years past is that they just don't know what to expect when they get there. There's an intimidation factor, stepping into a real-world game for the first time, not knowing how you'll be accepted face-to-face by the other players. And when you're just learning how to play and which hands to play, the veil of anonymity online gives timid people the courage to dive into the poker pond, whereas, if it were a face-to-face game, they'd just never go near the water.

I believe many players will learn to excel at poker who might otherwise never have played the game. It's all because of the online poker opportunity.

REASON #5.
DON'T NEED TO DRESS UP OR GROOM

I got to thinking—there are times when you like to dress up and times when you don't. I try to look my best when I go to church, go to a social function, or go to a decent restaurant with my family. It makes me feel better about myself.

But there are times when I'd rather be flat-out comfortable and I don't care if I'm dressed to impress. One of those times is when I'm playing poker. Unless I'm being filmed, I'm less choosey about what I wear to a poker game. Of course, I dress reasonably well, even then, because I think some of the attire seen at the poker tables is a downright disgrace and reflects poorly on our game. But, basically, I don't overdo it.

The truth is, though, if it weren't for how others might view me, I'd rather not bother about how I look when I play poker. And online play gives me the opportunity to dress anyway I like. As many have noted, you can play poker online in your pajamas and no one will care. Now, that's definitely a bonus you get *only* when playing poker by computer.

REASON #6.
HEADS-UP CHALLENGES

If you like to play heads-up, online cardrooms are beginning to provide previously unavailable opportunities. Have you ever wondered why there are so few heads-up matches in real-world casinos? Surely, heads-up can't be that unpopular, because just the thought of a high-intensity one-on-one game can make pulses race. And isn't it the final heads-up hands in a tournament that are the most exciting to watch on television? Let me tell you, having enjoyed a lot of experience in this situation, those final heads-up hands are not just the most exciting to *watch*—they're also the most exciting to play!

So why aren't heads-up games available in cardrooms and casinos? It's because those games are not economical for them. Each game takes up valuable real estate—a full table. Worse, each game requires a dealer—who is hired to provide service to up to 10 players at a table—just to service two customers.

But online, this all changes. It costs nothing to set up a new table for two players, because the tables are purely imaginary, just tiny dots forming the image on your computer monitor. And online casinos don't worry about you using up their tables, because they can provide as many as they want at no cost. No tables to purchase. No cardroom floor space limitations. But, bigger than that is the fact that online poker doesn't worry about paying dealers. The cards are all shuffled and distributed by the software. There's no cost involved in dealing more cards or adding more games.

That's why I believe you're going to see a surge in heads-up play online. There's another reason why some players might choose heads-up online. They fear collusion, but that's not really as much of an issue as you'd think, which I'll explain later in this chapter.

Still, for those who don't trust situations where they're playing against multiple opponents that they can't physically scrutinize, heads-up play might just be the answer. One opponent can't collude. However, to me, that isn't an issue. Online games can be monitored in ways so sophisticated that they'd shock those who aren't technically schooled and even the most knowledgeable computer wizards. While I enjoy short-handed games, and even heads-up, I'm very comfortable against multiple opponents and sometimes prefer to play against a full table of online opponents.

Heads-up is a war of egos. And only online can you sit in London and play a hotly contested match against an opponent in Australia sitting on his bed with a laptop computer.

REASON #7.
MORE HANDS PER HOUR

When online poker first debuted in the late nineties, poker rooms actually built in a delay to simulate the time it took to deal cards in the real world. Boy, was that a mistake! It quickly became apparent that players didn't want the delays. The faster their cards arrived, the happier they were. That's why doylesroom.com and most other online rooms have taken all the "air" out of dealing and shuffling. There is *no* delay.

Because of that, you play many more hands per hour online. In most cases, it's about twice as many as you'd play in the real world. That means that if you're a winning player you can make more money faster. Each hand you play is worth money when you're playing the way I advise in this book, and twice the hands can mean up to twice the profit.

REASON #8.
PLAY TWO OR MORE GAMES AT ONCE

You see some pretty weird things at poker. I've seen players hold seats at adjoining tables and scurry back and forth, trying to play both games for short periods of times. This usually happens when the player has "free" hands remaining before the blind at one game and has been called to a seat from the waiting list for another game. Needless to say, playing two games at once in the real world doesn't work well. It's physically impractical, and you're almost certain to be rude by delaying the play of a hand at one table, while completing action at another.

But, online, it's much simpler to enter a second, third, or even more games. When it's your turn to act, the software notifies you—and you simply click to fold, call, check, or raise. Since you don't have to get out of your seat and physically move to the other table, multiple game play becomes practical online.

Does this mean more profit for you? It can—if you're good enough. Try to remember, though, that you won't be able to focus as closely on multiple games as you would on a single game. You'll miss some of the nuances and won't be able to track your opponents' tendencies as readily. That means your average earnings per game are sure to suffer when you play multiple games simultaneously. But, when you add those slightly diminished profits from multiple games together, you'll probably find that you'll earn more money altogether. Whether you do or not, of course, depends on your skills.

I recommend that you stick to just one game at first, because it can be quite hectic concentrating on two or more at the same time. But, as you get accustomed to playing multiple games, you might find it exciting and rewarding. Certainly, there's no equivalent to this in real-world poker.

REASON #9.
EARLY ACTION OR PRE-SELECT BUTTONS

One of the great inventions of online poker is the early action or pre-select buttons. These buttons are an ingenious invention that leverages the fact that online, you can secretly tell the software what your next action will be, before it's your turn to act! Since your opponents are sitting in their own homes, possibly on the other side of the planet, they have no idea which button you've decided to push.

In real-world poker, pre-selecting wouldn't be appropriate, because that would let opponents who act before you know how you planned to respond.

The early action choices help speed up the play—and they're especially useful if you're playing other games simultaneously. For instance, when you know you're going to fold, no matter what, you can just click the "Fold" button before the action gets to you and concentrate on a different table, where you hold a more promising hand.

Limit Pre-Select Buttons

Here's an example from Doyle's Room:

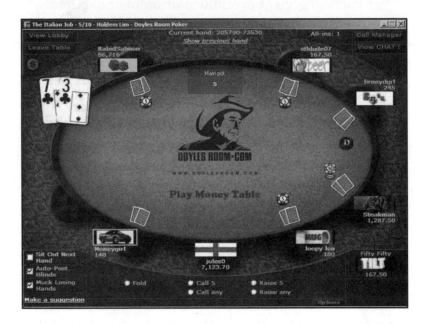

Imagine your player name is "Fifty Fifty." You're holding the 7-3 of clubs on the left side of the table. It's a straight limit game, and you're waiting for Moneygirl at the bottom of the screen to act. But you don't have to wait until it's your turn to make a decision. Look at the bottom of the screen. You can click right now—"Fold," "Call 5," "Call any," "Raise 5," or "Raise any."

The pre-select options change, depending on whether the game is limit or no-limit and what your choices are at the time. If it's after the flop and nobody has bet, your pre-select options will be different that those just shown.

They might look like this, instead:

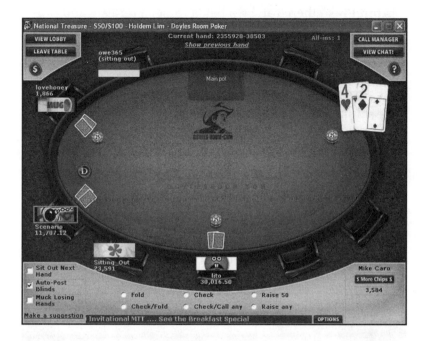

Here, there's no opportunity for a call, since you're in the big blind (upper right) with 4♥ 2♦ and nobody has raised yet. You can see that there's a "Check/Fold" button, as well as a "Check/Call" button. **Check/Fold** means that you will check if no one bets and fold if someone does. It's an especially important button, because when opponents use it often, you can sometimes gain information, as I'll soon explain.

Check/Call means you will check if no one bets, but if someone bets, you'll call. This applies to only the first bet. That pre-selected action will be canceled if there's a reraise.

There's also the **Raise any** button. This means to keep raising as many times as you can until the maximum number of bets is reached. At Doyle's Room and most other sites, that maximum number of raises in limit games is three—so there can be a bet, a raise, a reraise, and one final reraise, and that's it. Beyond that point, players can only call; they cannot make further raises unless it's heads-up, where unlimited raises are allowed.

No-Limit Pre-Select Buttons

Here's an example, from a no-limit game, of what your choices would look like when there is a bet...

In no-limit games, you'll find a more restricted choice of pre-select buttons, simply because there's no fixed amount for a raise. If you decide to raise, you'll have to enter an amount, so raising isn't included as an early choice.

I'll discuss early action buttons more under the list of online poker tips, and you'll learn some surprising advantages you can enjoy using these buttons.

REASON #10.
RANDOM SHUFFLES

Some players doubt whether the shuffle in online poker is as random as in real-world games. In fact, online shuffles are more random than real-world shuffles. The science of simulating random events, including card distribution, is well advanced and it's impossible for a human dealer to even come close to shuffling cards with the same random distribution.

Another advantage with computerized shuffling and dealing is that you won't have any misdeals. Nor will cards be inadvertently flashed, one of the common irritations of real-world poker.

REASON #11.
RAKES ARE ACTUALLY LESS

At the higher limits I play in real-world casinos, pots are seldom raked. Instead there's an hourly seat rental. But, most everyday limits, through $10/$20 and often higher, are raked. If you're looking for a bargain, you'll find that those rakes are a little less online.

REASON #12.
NO TIPPING

It's customary to tip the dealer when you win a pot. It's not mandatory, but most players do it. In a $5/$10 game, you might throw a dollar the dealer's way whenever you win a pot with any size to it. The dealers make most of their income from these tips, because they're paid at very low base wages. These dollars you tip add up, and you could buy some nice Christmas presents at the end of the year if you didn't have to pay them. Well, online, you don't. In fact, you *can't*, because there is no real dealer to appreciate or accept your gesture.

But, I had a strange thought. Players being as supersti- tious as they are, I'm wondering if Doyle's Room should add an optional "Tip" button. I believe so many players would choose to tip the non-existant dealer that I might waive my endorsement fee and get rich off those tips.

REASON #13.
POKER CLOCK

In poker, an opponent can't stall forever, whether it's an everyday game or a tournament. Although it's rare, you'll sometimes see a player take a long time before acting on a hand. Now, in no-limit play, this is occasion- ally acceptable. Decisions can have extreme importance, and a player needs time to think about the situation and study his opponent.

But, even in no-limit, most players act more quickly than you'd expect. It's a rare hand when they take a lot of time to ponder. And in limit games, it's downright rude to waste time over and over again when the action gets to you. I believe, if you know you're going to fold, then you should usually just fold. Don't make a show of it.

Timing-Out Issue

Sometimes players take so long that if you allowed them to stall forever, the game would come to a halt. That's why in real-world poker, you can always ask to "put the clock" on an opponent. That gives him a set amount of time to complete the decision. Failure to act constitutes a fold.

The problem with that system is you don't want to be needlessly rude to opponents. Maybe they really do need the time. Maybe they're losing and confused. Maybe they're daring you to ask for the clock, so they can be hostile in return. Who knows?

The good thing about online poker is that it takes the awkward decision about asking for the clock out of your hands. If a player doesn't click on a decision button, after ten seconds or so he'll be prompted to do so. Some sites provide a countdown clock; Doyle's Room—in addition—has chosen gentle chimes to warn that you have 10 seconds left to act. What happens if you don't act online differs from cardroom to cardroom and situation to situation. If you haven't put any money in the pot, your hand will be folded. If you have, you'll usually be treated as if you're *already* all-in—in other words, you won't be able to make further bets into the pot—even though you still have chips in front of you. So you'll be left competing for a partial pot.

The Artificial All-In

Unscrupulous players sometimes try to use the "all-in" feature unfairly to their advantage. They'll pretend to have Internet communications problems, not realizing that most sites can tell that they're actually still connected. Sometimes they'll succeed in getting a free shot at part of a pot, when they would otherwise have folded.

That's why most sites only allow one or two artificial all-ins to be used per session, beyond which hands are folded, no matter what. That's also why players who abuse the treat-as-all-in privilege are suspended or barred.

Despite this hard-to-deal-with "timed-out" issue, unique to online poker, the presence of an automatic clock is an advantage that keeps the games moving swiftly. It's part of the reason why there are so many more hands dealt to you each hour online.

REASON #14.
MORE HANDS ALLOW LUCK TO EVEN OUT QUICKER

In most games of skill, the right decisions are quickly rewarded. In poker, the right decisions can cause misery in the short term. If you're not prepared for the frustrations that go with quick changes in fate, you don't have the right temperament to be a professional poker player.

Although superior players win in the long run, and you hardly ever hear about any full-time pros having a losing year, it's not hard to spend weeks or even a month suffering a net loss. But the longer you play, the more quickly that familiar "law of probability" takes hold, and the closer your results get to what really *should* happen.

But, even though we talk about chance taking time to even out, it really doesn't take a lot of *time*; it takes a lot of hands. What if you could get all those hands played in a short time? Well, suddenly, when you're playing online instead of in a physical casino, you're playing a lot more hands. The deals are amazingly brisk. The action is swift.

You can expect to get twice as many hands played each hour. And that's if you only play at a single table. Many winning players regularly play two or three games at once. That's up to six times as many hands per hour!

What does this mean in terms of a bad streak? It means that a run of losses that would have droned on for six days might stop after only one day. For certain, things will even out faster online. So, if you're a superior poker player, you can expect to win more consistently on a week-to-week basis when you play online.

REASON #15.
TOURNAMENTS ON DEMAND

Being able to play tournaments anytime, day or night, is among online poker's greatest advantages. You might see scheduled events at three in the morning, so, if you happen to be awake, dive right in. Why so early? Remember that poker is now a worldwide sport, and when it's early in the morning for you, it's afternoon somewhere else.

But, if tournaments scheduled around the clock isn't enough for you, try the unscheduled ones! There's a fast-and-furious form of tournament poker — the single-table shootout. You play down to one winner, with second and third place finishers also receiving money. It's the same as those popular one-table satellites that annoyed me by drying up the side action years ago at the major tournaments. The difference online is that you're playing for cash, not for a seat into a larger tournament. You can also play in regularly scheduled tournaments where the prize is a seat into major live tournaments, plus cash and travel expenses.

Sit and Goes

There's no scheduled starting time for these tournaments, which is why the popular name for them today has become **Sit and Goes** or **SNG's**. You take a seat at the table—by clicking to put your name on the list—and as soon as all the seats are filled, the cards automatically get dealt and the tournament begins. A table often fills in a matter of a minute or two.

You can put your name on other SNG lists and then play several of these tournaments at a time. SNG's usually take less than an hour—and a typical player will last about twenty minutes, on average, sometimes being eliminated almost immediately, sometimes surviving long enough to win. You can play SNG's all day, if this is your favorite poker form—they're always available.

REASON #16.
MORE COMFORTABLE
THAN A CROWDED TABLE

I hate sitting elbow to elbow. I'm a big man—at least I was until my recent gastric bypass surgery—and you can imagine how important it has been, throughout my poker career, to have enough room to feel comfortable. In the real world, I usually play short-handed, but when I have to crowd into a nine- or ten-hand game, as I do for tournaments, I'm always wishing for more space. Online, I don't worry about that. I can play from a recliner with a keyboard in my lap, if I want to, and still be at a full table.

REASON #17.
YOU CAN PLAY FOR VERY SMALL LIMITS

In my mind, making small-limit poker available to players is online poker's greatest contribution to our game. Personally, I don't think of $2 and $4 games as meaningful limits. But for players who are just starting out and on a small bankroll, the difference between a $50 win and a $50 loss can be significant. Those small limits can actually be uncomfortable for players just learning the game.

One great idea that has been made possible by online poker rooms is to have formal games where beginners could make bets for as little as 10 cents. These games allow neophytes who are too timid to risk meaningful money at poker to get comfortable with the game, players who would otherwise never experience the thrill of poker in a casino.

As I pointed out earlier, real-world casinos can't afford to do this, because of the costs involved in providing physical tables and paying human dealers. But online poker rooms can and do make this great contribution.

REASON #18.
PLAY POKER FOR FREE!

And why not take this advantage of being able to economically spread online games a step further? Why not offer just-for-fun games for those who aren't ready to play poker "for keeps"?

Most online poker rooms, including DoylesRoom.com, do exactly that. They let players learn the mechanics of the game by playing for imaginary money. And they charge nothing for this promotional service to the poker community. Real-world casinos can't afford to do that.

I wouldn't be surprised if many successful real-world players, and even future World Poker Tour, World Series of Poker, and other champions, will launch their careers on free online tables.

REASON #19.
QUALIFY ONLINE FOR
REAL-WORLD TOURNAMENTS

I was skeptical of the value of online poker a few years ago. So were many of the people who managed real-world cardrooms. They were afraid that online poker would siphon off their business, more than it would help bring in new players to their physical cardrooms.

That argument has been resolved. Today, it's hard to find anyone in the industry who doesn't realize that online games have helped in the resurgence of real-world poker. I meet players everyday at the Bellagio, Commerce, and elsewhere who began playing poker online.

And the one argument that proves the point most convincingly is the number of players at the major tournaments who qualified online. For some, these real-world tournaments constitute their first exposure to casino poker. They like the adventure of playing against live opponents they actually can shake hands with and speak to at the tables. And they enjoy trying to read them and spot tells—something that isn't possible online.

Count the new players pouring into casino poker tournaments through online channels, and you'll be as convinced as I am that online poker has greatly helped to bring our game into the public spotlight, giving it the respect it always deserved, but never had until recently.

REASON #20.
OPTIONAL FOUR-COLOR DECKS

I've got to confess. I've never been a fan of four-color decks. With the traditional deck of cards I grew up with, hearts and diamonds are both red, and spades and clubs are both black. They tell me that four-color decks, with each suit having its own color, were tried over a hundred years ago. Apparently, it wasn't as economical to print them that way, and two colors became the custom.

I prefer two-color decks, because that's what I'm used to. But, there's obviously a strong argument for a four-color deck. It makes it much easier to spot flushes and flush possibilities at a glance. When Mike Caro publicly started making a big deal about changing to four-colors ten years ago, I thought he was goofy. He tried unsuccessfully to introduce four-color decks to real-world casinos, even going so far as promoting a "C-Day," for Color Deck Day where this novelty was introduced to sixty-five casinos simultaneously.

The effort fell flat, because poker players don't like change and because the differences in colors that he chose were too subtle to be easily distinguished across the table. Old timers like me balked, while on the other hand, many beginners liked the decks. It would have been nice if everyone could play with the deck they preferred, but that was obviously impossible. You had to choose one or the other, and the traditional two-color deck continued to rule in real-world casinos.

Online, it's different. You *can* play with the deck of your choice. That's because the deck you choose is only displayed on your own computer screen. Your opponent can be looking at a different deck, and it won't make any difference to either one of you. That's why four-color decks have gained a new lease on life online—and only online, so far.

REASON #21.
SOFTWARE TELLS YOU
WHEN IT'S YOUR TURN

You've had this happen before. A player sits patiently, because he doesn't realize it's his turn. You sit patiently, too, because you don't want to be rude while, you assume, he's making a decision. Yes, we've all seen this impasse time and again.

Online, this awkward moment never happens. The software prods players for a decision, letting them know precisely when it's their turn to act.

REASON #22.
NO STIGMA ABOUT
LEAVING A GAME EARLY

I believe that a player should never need to provide a reason for leaving a game. The common notion that you're being unfair if you sit down for a short time and leave with a big profit is nonsense. In poker, you put your money at risk. If you win, it's your money, and you can get up and leave anytime you feel like it.

Still, this is sometimes hard to do in the real-world. If you "hit and run" too often, you're apt to get a reputation as the type of player some don't like to play against. It never bothers me when players win and leave quickly, but it does bother others. Personally, I usually prefer to play longer sessions, but I don't frown on those who'd rather play short ones.

Online, you won't encounter any stigma when you take the money and run. Opponents realize that you might only have ten minutes to play right then, and you can just click "Leave Table" and be out of the game without fanfare or making excuses. In fact, you need to pay attention to even notice who comes and goes in a game, because it happens so quickly online. If you're one of those players who likes to play short sessions and leave with your winnings intact, online play is your kind of poker. For the most part, nobody cares or even notices.

REASON 23.
DATABASE HELPS MAINTAIN GAME INTEGRITY

Sometimes players are worried about competing against partnerships, because they've heard that opponents might be on the phone sharing information about each other's hands in order to gang up on honest players.

Now, while collusion is always something to be alert to—whether you're playing poker online or in the real world—the fact is that online poker has an advantage: The software keeps a database of every hand ever played. Also, many of the best sites have automated software that red-flags suspicious behavior for experienced humans to investigate further. And if management is the least bit suspicious, it can go back in time and look at every relevant hand played for players suspected of colluding.

If players decide to team up and play their best hands, or if they try any other irregular tricks, it's usually easy to spot.

And, what about one player trying to pose as several players by using multiple computers out of one location? That person is in double jeopardy of getting caught, because not only do sites have databases to check for collusion, they can determine when communications are coming from the same location.

THE INTEGRITY OF
REAL-WORLD POKER

Real-world surveillance and game protection has also improved dramatically in recent years. I'm certain that, on average, poker is more honest today than it's been at any time in history. If you doubt this, just look at the players who are regularly winning the major tours. They tend to be models of class and integrity.

But it isn't the big names who always win. Sometimes, the winners are unknown players—some rank amateurs. That, in itself, testifies to the integrity of real-world poker today.

Of course, some players will try to take unethical shots at online poker, but you'd be surprised how little they succeed online. This was one of my biggest concerns when I first thought about online poker. And, to be sure, no game is ever perfectly safe or perfectly protected. It's the responsibility of honest players to report instances that make them suspicious. I always recommend that you leave a game if you don't trust it. Even if your suspicions turn out to be unmerited, you won't drive yourself crazy if you happen to get on a long losing streak.

But, overall, with the database and other modern-age computer techniques, you can feel reasonably safe playing poker online. Collusion is easier to spot than in real-world casinos, even though everywhere poker is more honest than it's ever been.

In my mind, this built-in security gives online poker an advantage over real-world poker.

REASON #24:
YOU WON'T GET ROBBED

One thing about playing online that bigger-limit players might find appealing is that you're not going to get robbed. That might not sound like a big issue to casual players, but most high-limit professionals can tell you a dozen horror stories about carrying around large sums of cash. In Super/System, I talk about an experience I had being the victim of a home invasion robbery when coming home from the World Series of Poker.

Online, you don't worry about that. All transactions are handled electronically. So, if someone barges into your home with a gun, they won't get your cash—at least not the chips you have on the table.

♠♥♦♣

Powerful Game Strategies

Now, I'll give you some basic advice about how to win at poker. Almost everything in this book applies. Online poker *is* real poker.

Keep in mind how I advise playing against bad players, because you can just assume most of the players you'll confront online are bad. Or, at least, you'll find yourself up against more unsophisticated and loose players than you will in real-world casinos.

PLAY STRAIGHTFORWARD POKER

The trick to beating games filled with weak players is to avoid doing anything fancy. You don't need to. Most of your profit will come from choosing to do the obvious right thing. Raise when raising is your logical first choice. Fold when your hands are weak. Bluff sparingly in limit games. Against the type of player you meet online, you should try fewer tricks than you would in the real world.

Online, you'll find that opponents are treating poker a little more like bingo, paying attention to their own hands mostly and paying attention to you only a little or not at all. Creative players will have trouble adapting to the reality of online poker. That's because creative plays often sacrifice profit, rather than enhancing it.

In short, when you're playing online, make obvious, strong decisions. Don't try to be too fancy. Your efforts to confuse opponents will often be wasted, because without your physical presence, they're not paying as much attention to what you do.

BET NORMAL AMOUNTS

The value of making unusual bets in no-limit games is reduced online. Some players like to fool around with the sizes of their bets. For instance, instead of betting $1,000, they'll throw $1,025 or $975 in chips into a pot, but I think it's pretty much a waste of time. I'm skeptical about whether this has much affect even in real-world games where opponents are apt to take notice. But, online, players are *not* apt to pay much attention to the exact amount of the bet. They're just clicking buttons in response, so they don't have to physically count out $1,025 or $975 to call. For that reason, I believe you should seldom bet strange amounts online. It just slows down the game when you have to type in the amount.

Since the way to get the most money online is to act swiftly and make the obvious plays, there's usually not as much motivation to do unusual things.

SEVEN POWERFUL PLAYS AND MANEUVERS

Following are seven powerful plays and maneuvers that are applicable to almost any variation of poker. Each is a weapon that should be kept handy in your poker arsenal. The advice below shows what adjustments you should make from regular games to online, if any. The strategies are specific to either limit or no-limit games *if* stated. Otherwise, the strategies apply to both forms of the game.

1. ROBBING THE BLINDS

Real-World Play: Rob the blinds often against conservative opponents.

Online Play: Rob the blinds sometimes against conservative opponents, but generally less often. The big blind calls more often online.

2. CALLING AS THE SMALL BLIND

Real-World Play: You should usually call if no one else has raised, except with total garbage hands.

Online Play: Same online.

3. CHECKING AND RAISING (GENERAL)

Real-World Play: Use this frequently as a weapon against observant opponents.

Online Play: Use much less frequently online. Since many players keep betting weakly, just check and keep calling. The best time to check-raise is on the river, when you can't discourage any future betting, anyway. Until, then, you'll find many opportunities to let opponents "hang themselves" online.

4. SHOWING A WEAK HAND

Real-World Play: Seldom do it. Many players consider it insulting to show a weak hand after you've bluffed successful, and you can spoil the friendly atmosphere that brings profit. Once in a while, it's okay, if you're sure your opponent is in a playful mood and will take it gracefully.

Online Play: Show weak bluffs much more often *if* you think it will help you get future calls. Online players are much less likely to be offended, because you don't have a physical presence to be mad at.

5. RERAISING

Real-World Play: You do this for two reasons: (1) Because you have the best hand; (2) To leverage position so that players check into you on the next betting round.

Online Play: Same online.

6. BLUFFING ON EARLY BETTING ROUNDS

Real-World Play: Profitable against sophisticated opponents.

Online Play: Also profitable, but you need to be more selective, because most opponents will call more often—all the way to the river. They call more readily online, because there's less of an embarrassment factor in having to explain themselves face-to-face to other players.

7. SLOWPLAYING STRONG HANDS BY LETTING OTHERS BET FOR YOU

Real-World Play: An occasional tool, as long as you don't overuse it.

Online Play: Use this tool more often online, because players are less observant of individual opponents, letting you reuse the same profitable tactic again and again.

TWO MORE CONCEPTS
SANDBAGGING

Let me settle a dispute about **sandbagging** which is checking and then raising if an opponent bets after you check. Some players, particularly those unfamiliar with how standard poker is played, think it's unethical to check and then raise.

But, in my whole career as a poker player, I never met a professional, serious opponent, or fan of the game who thought there was anything wrong with sandbagging. The tactic is a traditional weapon in poker. It makes it harder for an opponent to bet medium hands after you check, because he fears he might encounter a raise.

Remember, the last player to act has a positional advantage, getting to see what others do first. So, it just plain makes sense that a tactic that partially equalizes that advantage is a part of poker. Without the ability to sandbag, poker strategy can get seriously out of balance in favor of the player acting last.

But even if sandbagging doesn't feel quite right to you, try to get used to it. There's hardly a casino you can visit in the real world where sandbagging is forbidden. And, online, I know of no site that forbids it.

125

Yet, every once in a while a player complains about it—particularly a beginner. That player will soon be set straight by others in the game.

Whether you're playing hold'em, draw poker, or whatever form of the game online, it's always okay and always perfectly ethical to sandbag. There's nothing un-friendly about it. Of course, you can't sandbag on the first betting round if there's a blind bet involved. A blind bet means the pot is already opened and your only choices are to raise, call, or fold.

But, even in blind games, it makes sense to occasion-ally sandbag on the later rounds of betting, when nobody is forced to wager. I'm really telling you this to make sure you have the right attitude to play online. Whether it's sandbagging or anything else, don't let your feelings overshadow your good judgment.

The standard tactics in poker exist for a reason. You can choose to use them or not, but you shouldn't criticize someone else for using them. But, some players do get angry for the silliest reasons, and their attitude tends to spoil the game.

A WORD ON BLUFFING

If you get bluffed out of a pot, don't take it personally. Bluffing is part of the fun of the game. We all get bluffed out of pots regularly. And if someone gets lucky and beats you, don't tell them they played bad and instill hostility into the game. Be a bigger person and move on.

If you don't spoil the game for others, you'll enjoy it more yourself. So, I guess that's a tip—keep the game pleasant and you'll probably fare better. At least, you'll feel better about yourself. And when you feel better about yourself, others feel better toward you. Then it's a happier world of poker. And you're doing your part to popularize the game in a way you might not have realized.

Winning Game Strategies

I need to remind you that this isn't a book on poker strategy. It's a book intended to get you familiar with the idea of playing poker online, to show the advantages and disadvantages, and to suggest ways you might modify your real-world strategy when you play poker on your computer. If you're looking to learn poker at the root level, there are many excellent books. When you're ready to tackle winning seriously, I recommend my twin books *Super/System — A Course in Power Poker*, published in 1978, and *Super/System 2*, published in 2005.

Still, I want to give a smattering of tips I believe may help you. Some are aimed at novices, because I know a lot of readers will just be beginning their poker journey. Others are more sophisticated.

Here they are:

SELECTED HOLD'EM TIPS

1. PLAY SMALL PAIRS CAUTIOUSLY

You'll get gobbled up alive, whether you're playing online or in a traditional casino, if you treat a pair in hold'em the same way you would in seven-card stud. In seven-card stud, *any* pair is *something*. It has potential not only because it can combine to make three-of-a-kind, but because it often wins by simply improving to two-pair.

When you have one small pair in seven-card stud, the key to overtaking your opponent and winning the hand is catching another pair. Surely, it must sound strange to experienced players that beginners don't realize that they can't catch a new pair on board and catch up in hold'em. But, I'm betting that at one point most of the sophisticated players didn't realize it, either. Some experienced players no doubt overrate small pairs after years of play.

The reason you can't help by catching another pair on board in hold'em is that, if you're already behind, that new pair will also help your opponent. It will belong to everyone equally. So, if you start with a pair of fours in hold'em and a pair of tens land on the board, you "improved" from one pair to two pair, but it didn't help you at all.

Usually, you'll play small pairs in limit games if you can get in for a single bet behind many callers. Then you're either going to catch three-of-a-kind or surrender to a bet. You should usually fold from early positions if aggressive players are likely to raise. That holds true for limit or no-limit games.

The best tactic when you hold a small pair, meaning sixes on down (but medium pairs are vulnerable, too) is to attack the blinds, call in the blinds, or to get in the pot cheaply in hopes of making three of a kind. Do not overplay this hand.

2. DON'T OVERPLAY SUITED CONNECTORS

Suited connectors are two cards of adjacent rank in the same suit, neither too high nor too low, thus giving room to breathe and expand into a straight more easily. For that reason, when a seasoned player talks about suited connectors, he usually means hands ranging from J-10 suited to 6-5 suited and seldom any hands higher or lower. I'd like you to take a look at the four hands right in the middle of that spectrum...

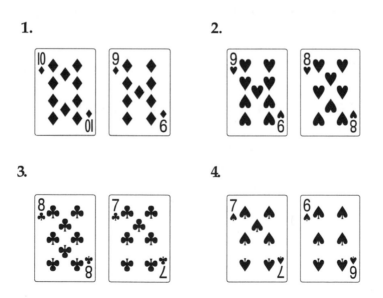

Of course, these hands can be any suit, as long as both cards are the *same* suit. I believe suited connectors tend to be overplayed in limit games, especially when the action is likely to leave you against a few aggressive players. You really want to see a lot of players and no raises, so you can take your shot cheaply.

There's no disgrace in folding suited connectors. It's highly possible that players with only average abilities beyond the flop lose money overall by playing them. If you fold, it's usually no big sacrifice—especially for beginners. But if you play them unwisely, it can mean a serious leak in your game. And, I'm politely suggesting that you examine your own play to make certain you don't have that leak.

The way I feel about it, these hands have much more profit potential in no-limit games than in limit games. If you come in cheaply in a no-limit game and you get lucky enough to connect—which is rare—you have the potential to snare a very large pot. That grand slam possibility doesn't exist in limit games.

3. CREATE AN AGGRESSIVE IMAGE

Whether you're playing limit or no-limit hold'em, you'll want an aggressive image to succeed. And the main time to create that image and to actually play aggressively is when you're involved in late-position combat. I like to go that extra bet or raise when I'm playing in late position.

4. SECURE POSITION WHEN POSSIBLE

In hold'em—unlike in seven-card stud, where your position on a given betting round is determined by the exposed cards—if you're the closest position clockwise to the dealer button at the end of the first betting round, you're going to keep that position throughout *all* the betting rounds. This is an important consideration and you'd do well to heed what I'm telling you. And that is that you need to secure position whenever you can do it.

You might think that putting in an extra raise with a fairly strong, but not sensational hand, is costly. But as often as not, that raise is actually productive and profitable if you're in a late position one or two seats in front of the button. If those key positions fold, you got position and leverage throughout the remainder of the hand.

So, when I'm faced with a fence-straddling hand that looks pretty powerful, but possibly not quite powerful enough to justify a raise, I'm often going to raise anyway in the last two seats before the button.

5. SELDOM CALL TWO OR MORE PLAYERS ON THE FLOP HOLDING ONLY OVERCARDS

In limit hold'em games, I'll frequently call heads-up after the flop with just two overcards. But if there is more than one opponent, I seldom will, unless I have either A-K or an additional inside straight draw.

The problem with calling with overcards other than A-K—and I won't always do it with that hand, either—is that you could connect and still lose pretty easily. For instance:

My Hand:

The Flop:

In this situation, I'm almost never going to call a bet unless I'm the only other player in the pot. To be candid, I might sometimes *raise!* But that's only if I think there's a better than average probability that the bettor is bluffing or weak. I just don't want to chase this one down with a call, because even if the next card brings a king or a jack, I could—in the case of a king—be trailing with hands like this...

  **OR**

And—in the case of a jack—I could be trailing...

Even if I'm good, I still have to hope that an ace or a queen doesn't turn up on the river. Even if a king lands, I still need to worry about an ace landing.

In short, it's tough enough to make this call with the ultimate overcards, K-Q. You just can't expect to make a long-range profit by calling routinely against more than one opponent with lesser overcards. Throw that out of your playbook.

6. SELDOM SLOWPLAY BIG FLOPS AGAINST TIMID OPPONENTS

Timid opponents tend to be callers and not value bettors or bluffers. The best strategy against them is usually to bet aggressively. It's players who bluff quite often and those who have a fancy style of play that I tend to check into when I make a big flop. You can occasionally make exceptions, but generally that's the way I recommend you play it, too.

Oddly, some players who would otherwise be very credible have the bad habit of calling with overcards much too often. It's bewildering to see, and I hope you won't fall into that pitiful poker trap.

7. ONLINE HOLD'EM STRATEGY ADJUSTMENTS

The strategies that may make sense to follow in real-world games need to be adjusted for online play. As an example, if I'm playing hold'em in the real world, I'm very likely to raise with 9♣ 8♦ from the dealer position if everyone else has folded.

If the players in the blinds are aggressive, I'll likely just fold. But, if they aren't, and if I think I can dominate and make up ground on the following betting rounds, I'll dive right in, head first. Maybe I'll take the pot right then, picking up the blinds, or maybe I'll stumble into a good hand and maximize my surprise advantage. Also, I'll often get a good read on my opponents later on in the hand and get an opportunity to bluff profitably.

But, when I'm playing online, I usually just fold that same hand. I know that players tend to call more routinely online. I also know that I won't be able to manipulate them with subtle psychology. By subtle psychology, I don't mean putting on a show the way some other top players do. That's not my style. My type of manipulation is more that of a faint smile or just long-established intimidation that can be conveyed in ways that are impossible online.

Aggressive Online Plays

Online, I realize that opponents are playing their cards more and people less. There will be none of the physical tells that guide me to profit in my real-world game. So, to a great extent, I need to fall back to a powerful basic game plan. I vary from it much less online than I do in the real world of face-to-face poker.

Likewise, in limit games which tend to dominate online play, I'm less likely to reraise in a middle position against a raise immediately to my right with a hand like K-J suited than I would in a physical casino.

All my poker-playing career, I've tended to mix this up—sometimes just calling, sometimes raising.

And I might drive out hands that are clearly superior to mine, such as...

OR

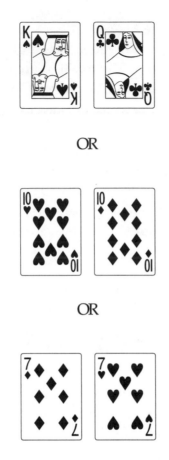

The main goal in this raise is to secure the best position, chasing away hands that would otherwise act after I do. That way, I have the luxury of seeing what others do before I make my decision. As I said, I don't do this all the time in the real-world, but I do it often. I take the composition of my opponents into account when deciding when to raise and when to just call. But, my main point is this: I raise quite often and have throughout all the successful years I've been playing poker at the highest limits, facing down some of the toughest opponents alive.

EYEBALL TO EYEBALL

Online, though, I'm not really facing anyone down. I can't stare anyone eyeball to eyeball. I can't study them and discern their states of mind. For an old warrior like me, that's a big penalty to pay. And because I have no choice but to pay it, I steer clear of awkward poker situations where I would need to rely on my people skills and my instincts to win money.

This means with that same K-J suited online, in that same situation—where a middle-position player to my right has just finished raising—I'm usually going to just call. In a way, that hurts my heart and runs contrary to my nature. I like to raise; I like to dominate. But when I'm playing online, I realize that there's just no way I'm going to be able to exercise my expertise at reading people and manipulating them. So, I'm going to most likely just call.

But, even online, you need to use judgment. You can't routinely just call. You need to think about it. If the players behind you are sophisticated enough to lay down semi-large hands against a reraise and the player who just now raised is loose and unsophisticated, I'll still try to isolate him with that reraise. I know that there's lots of money to be made when you can force the situation to be heads-up with the last-to-act position against a lesser opponent. So, in that case, I tend to reraise, even if I am playing online.

YOU MUST ADJUST

If you're like me, the fact that you must adjust online, that you must forego many of the plays that give you leverage in the real world, won't sit well with you. It's a sad concession you need to make when you enter the

Internet poker arena. But millions upon millions of new players are joining those games yearly, probably many thousands of new players each day. They all add to the growing popularity of poker, and this skyrocketing popularity gives you enormous profit opportunity.

If you want that share of the poker pie, you're going to need to adjust. More often than not, that adjustment means sacrificing some of your more aggressive people plays and winning the money in more traditional, unimaginative ways. I'm sorry to have to tell you that, but it's a fact. A sorry excuse for a fact, perhaps, but a fact, for certain.

I also must warn you that it's easy to get carried away online. Staring at that computer screen can be hypnotizing. You'd think it would be easier to get up and take a break than in the real world, but players I've talked to have expressed the thought that they seem stuck to their chair. They intend to get up, but then the next hand is dealt and the next, and these hands come so quickly, so much more quickly than in the real world that there is little time to pause and reflect. You're apt to outstay your abilities, meaning that you can get tired and be playing worse than you think and not know it. That's when you should quit the game or at least take a walk. But most players don't.

You're probably wondering how I know that they don't. I know because I monitor games regularly. Occasionally, there are players sitting out, but the percentage of hands missed is much less than in the real-world games I'm accustomed to playing. I can only surmise that there's something more compelling about online play that won't let players "hang up the phone" on it. They keep playing. And when they leave the table, they seem to return so quickly that you sometimes wonder how they could have made a trip to the bathroom so quickly.

My theory is that the constant stream of action online gives no stepping off point. You think about getting up, but then the next hand is already in progress and you're involved in it, and then you forget your previous intent. That may not be the whole explanation, but I'm betting it's a big part of it.

USE YOUR COMMON SENSE

In contrast, if you only have a short time to play, you can do that. If you travel to a real-world casino to play, you're pretty much committed to staying for a while. I often sit down online and play just a few hands and leave. But that's usually because I realized in advance that I only had a few minutes to spare. Most players sit down under less time constraint. There's no pre-determined end time. And so they stay and stay, and their play deteriorates. You can see it happening. My advice is to treat online play with the same common sense you would real-world play, assuming your goal is to win.

Find the best games, sit down, and if things aren't promising, take a break or quit. It's so easy to let your brain turn to mush, and I don't want that to happen to you.

SUMMARY

Of course, this list of hold'em tips could go on and on, but that isn't the purpose of this book. I tried to select a few that would be helpful to you, particularly in your online play.

SELECTED SEVEN-CARD STUD TIPS

Since I decided to give you a few of my favorite tips for hold'em, I might as well throw in some for seven-card stud for good measure. As with the hold'em tips, these should be useful whenever you play in the real world *and* whenever you play online.

Don't forget that I'll be talking about ways to adjust online. So, you might want to modify some of these tactics to tailor your play to a physical game or to an online game—depending on which you're playing at the moment.

Here's some advice for seven-card stud.

1. DON'T OVERDO THE BETTING OF COME HANDS FOR DECEPTIVE PURPOSES

Come hand is a term used to describe a hand that has an opportunity to convert to a straight or a flush, but isn't yet complete. Many aggressive players like to bet these in seven-card stud, hoping opponents will figure them for an already-potent hand. This is a good tactic, and one I use quite often. But, you need to mix it up. If observant opponents see you doing this too often, they'll frequently raise. This has several bad implications.

For one, you'll lose the ability to steal pots when you make a small pair on the next card. When you sometimes bet come hands, your opponents know that you often can have *real* betting hands as well. If you pair on board, you're apt to take a large pot right then, with just that single pair. This possibility is something that can add substantially to your profit and make betting a come hand worthwhile. But if you bet come hands too frequently, opponents will start to call too often and this benefit will disappear.

You should also know that if the bet isn't deceptive, the whole purpose of the play is defeated. The best thing you can usually do with a come hand is get a free card. So, when you do the betting yourself, you're never going to get a free card for your straight or flush draw. Worse, if opponents catch on, they're going to raise and not only won't you get a free card, you'll be paying a double price to see if you can connect. That's counterproductive.

So, I'm cautioning you to steer clear of betting come hands too often in seven-card stud. It's a mistake made by even credible players. And it's one *you* can avoid.

2. CONSIDER YOUR SIDE CARD

Even beginners probably recognize that the rank of their "side card" matters some when they enter a pot with a small pair. **Side card** means the one among the three starting cards in stud that isn't a member of the pair.

Although beginners and inexperienced players might take the rank of that side card into consideration, I seriously doubt that they attach the importance to it that it deserves. For example, if you have a small buried pair, such as a 5-5 with a 7 showing, and exposed cards surrounding you of K, 10, 8, A, you're obviously in nowhere near as good a shape as if you begin with 5-5 and a Q showing, with exposed cards surrounding you of J, 10, 10, 2.

Down Cards:　　　　　　　　**Door Card:**

Cards Exposed in Other Player's Hands

Down Cards: **Door Card:**

Cards Exposed in Other Player's Hands

While that may seem obvious, you need to realize just how profound the difference is. The first instance is pitiful and will cost you a lot of money overall if you pursue that hand. The second instance has potential and if played correctly, is profitable, sometimes significantly profitable.

Yet, to some players, a pair of fives is seemingly a pair of fives, and a pair of threes is a pair of threes. I advise you to get in the habit of considering your side card—whether it's showing or buried—to be the most important determining factor in how you play a small starting pair in seven-card stud.

3. HOW OFTEN IS YOUR OPPONENT'S STARTING PAIR THE RANK OF HIS DOOR CARD?

Door card is a seven-card stud term meaning the face up card on the starting round. For each starting hand, two cards are facedown and **buried in the hole** and one card is face up for all to see.

Assuming you ignore all other cards you've seen, a lot has been made of the fact that if an opponent bets with exactly one pair, it's twice as likely to be the exact rank as his door card as to be a pair of mystery rank, buried in the hole.

I know how they reason this out, but there's a flaw in the logic. That "logic" is that if there's one pair among the first three cards, there are three ways it can be positioned. It could consist of cards #1 and #2, in which case it would be buried. Otherwise, it could consist of either card #1 and card #3 *or* card #2 and card #3. In either of those two cases, one member of the pair is exposed. So, the thinking goes, there's twice the chance that the pair being bet is of the rank showing.

In my experience, this doesn't pan out. The simple fact is that players are more likely to bet big pairs than small ones. So, if you see a conservative player with a four as his door card bet into big opposing cards, the chances aren't two out of three that he has a pair of fours.

The chances that he holds that small pair are sometimes almost nonexistent.

So, I'll admit that the chances are 2 to 1 in favor of the exposed pair if we're talking about just *having* it. But once the bet is flung out there, the odds are much different and you need to reevaluate the possibilities of what your opponent might hold in accordance with his playing style.

4. LOOK AROUND BEFORE PLAYING THAT THREE-FLUSH

Starting with three cards of the same suit can be profitable, but not always. First, the ranks of your cards matter greatly.

The truth is, when you start with a three-flush and win, it's *usually* not going to be with a flush! You might win with anything from a high card to four of a kind without catching two more of your cherished suit on the final four cards. That's why it's important to play most *high* ranking suited cards—cards that, if they pair, are likely to be competitive. Remember, that the ranks by themselves sometimes don't matter as much as how they compare to the cards you see around you. Of course, you want to be sensible about how you employ this advice, because there are twice as many cards dealt to opponents on their starting hands that you *don't* see as the ones you *do* see. But, in general, three suited cards like...

With opposing exposed cards like…

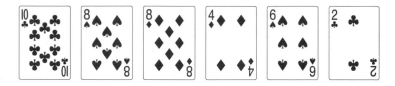

Are more likely to be profitable than these three suited cards…

With opposing exposed cards like…

The secret is that you want as many exposed as possible to be lower than most of your ranks. When that happens, you're less likely to make a pair that is beat by one your opponents either already have or might make later.

My son Todd has made his mark in the poker world, both in tournaments and by beating the biggest games in the world (once for millions of dollars in a single night). His success has been so phenomenal and his thoughtful poker observations so compelling that I included him as my expert on seven-card stud in *Super/System 2*. And one of the points he made in that book comes to mind now.

Todd pointed out that when you see *two* aces against you, most players instinctively worry less about facing a pair of aces, because they figure each of those opponents is handicapped by not being able to catch an ace. It's true that they're handicapped, but when you combine the *two* players chance of having one of the two remaining aces, it becomes more likely that one of those players has aces than a single player showing an ace would.

So, you don't want to see many cards ranking higher than most of your flush cards, even if you see two of that same rank. You want to see *lower* cards.

Keep this in your head: When you start with three flush cards led by a high card, and win, it's probably *not* going to be by making a flush. You're going to stumble your way into something else, and it will all center around pairing. That's why it's important that the ranks of your flush start are as high as possible relative to the cards you see exposed around you.

When you start with high suited cards, you often make pairs and two-pair that win; when you start with low suited cards, you often make pairs and two-pair that lose. That's why suited cards usually need to be high to be played.

Twenty-Five Online Poker Tips

ONLINE POKER TIP #1
CHOOSE THE RIGHT ICON

At a physical poker table, players are seeing the real you—or, at least, the "real you" that you're pretending to be. If you're more attuned to what your opponents are thinking than they are to what you're thinking, you'll have a chance to manipulate them.

Almost all the top players have an advantage in this area of psychology. Most seem to be naturally adept at getting inside their opponents heads and knowing how to behave at the very moment those players are thinking about calling, betting, raising, or folding. Sometimes it's awesome recognizing the power you hold over others, how you can sometimes sway them at the last moment to do what you'd like them to, just with a smile or a misleading gesture.

I'm not especially animated at the table, but I can manipulate in subtle ways. But, now, remember that the whole possibility of manipulating a poker opponent is based on the fact that they can see and hear you.

What if they can't? What if you're playing online?

Well, then the most obvious thing they'll relate to is your icon—so choose one wisely. Besides your screen name, it's how your opponents will come to recognize you. If you intend to play tight and want your opponents to think otherwise, represent yourself with an avatar that looks like a crazy or carefree person. If you want to play tight and take advantage of bluffing opportunities, I'd choose an avatar that is nondescript or that suggests a methodical person, perhaps one that looks like an accountant.

What if the site offers Monopoly-type icons that don't necessarily look like people? What if you choose from objects to represent you, as you do at Doyle's Room? Then a racehorse, a fast car, or almost anything silly looking might lead a few players to believe you're playing looser than you are. Something solid, like a stone or a brick might work to make a few people think you're tight and make it easier for you to bluff.

Yes, this is a stretch. In reality, the influence your icon has won't be earth shattering. But, since you're going to have to live with it day in and day out, it's worth your while to choose one that makes opponents think about you the way you'd like them to.

Pick an icon that that looks flamboyant or playful enough to encourage your opponents to call. If you want to bluff, choose an icon that sort of fades into the background and doesn't draw attention to itself. Who knows what's going to motivate an opponent to call? Nobody does for sure. But the more you draw attention to yourself in an online poker game, the more likely you are to find yourself a target of callers. And if your style of play is such that you make most of your money bluffing, don't pick an attention-getting icon.

ONLINE POKER TIP #2
USING ACTUAL PHOTOS FOR ICONS

By the way, some sites may allow you to use an actual photo of yourself. If your opponents are using these, I'd be suspicious, because I'm speculating that what you see isn't always what you get. If I see my opponent across the table represented by a photo of a beautiful woman in a revealing outfit, I'm wondering if that's Puggy Peason or some other world-class male player trying to play a trick on me. I wouldn't put it past them.

But, if you're ever playing on a site where you can use a photo, remember my previous tip. Pose for a new photo or choose one that conveys the image you want your opponents to see. If you want calls, make that pose wilder. If you want to bluff more, comb that hair and try to look like an accountant.

While the icon you choose may be the most visible indication of you when you play Internet poker, it's not the only thing that will influence your opponents. The screen name you choose will influence them, also.

ONLINE POKER TIP #3
YOUR SCREEN NAME MAY MATTER

If you're thinking that intelligent people won't usually be fooled by a screen name, you're right. But, despite people's conscientious attempts to keep from being swayed, they might occasionally be more inclined to call a player who presents himself with the screen name "Loose Larry" than if the name were "Tight Tony."

Of course, some players will react just the opposite. They're afraid of being conned and will consider the player to be temperamentally opposite of the chosen nickname. Sometimes that's a good way to consider an opponent and sometimes it isn't.

Although many intelligent players won't be fooled, enough players occasionally will be influenced by a playful or reckless sounding nickname so that you'll get more calls and earn more money—if calls are your primary goal. If you believe you'll make the most money by bluffing, than I'd recommend you choose a neutral-sounding screen name or even a conservative one, such as "Frugal Fred."

In online poker, where every extra edge helps, you should decide on a screen name that is most likely to influence your opponents the way you want, even if it only amounts to winning a few extra dollars now and then. By the way, it's been suggested to me that you might get dual advantages by choosing a loose-looking icon and a tight-sounding nickname or vice versa. I'm sure that might confuse the opposition, but I'm not convinced it would be effective, because you wouldn't know yourself what online image you were trying to convey.

ONLINE POKER TIP #4
DON'T CASH OUT TOO FREQUENTLY

While it's relatively easy to get cash into online games, it's still a lot harder than just reaching into your pocket and buying chips. I believe many players fare much worse online than they ought to, simply because they're short on money. If you get short playing good poker, that's one thing. But if you get short because you requested cash-outs when you really didn't need the money—well, you're just hamstringing yourself. I strongly recommend that you make it a practice to let your online bankroll grow until you feel fairly certain that you'll never lose it in a week of bad cards. Only then should you consider withdrawing some of your winnings.

Once you find an online cardroom that you trust and where you want to play, my advice is to keep enough money in your account so that you won't worry about going broke. Even if you have millions of dollars to gamble with, it's still stressful to be near the bottom of an online bankroll, knowing it will take some maneuvering to get more funds if you run out.

ONLINE POKER TIP #5
CHOOSE THE RIGHT GAME

In the days when I was traveling the Texas and Southern circuit, you could make choices. But they weren't the same game-selection choices available to casino players today. You see, there were seldom competing games of consequence on the same nights. There were some regular games, but mostly everyone knew where the best action was, and you either decided to play there or you didn't.

Well, along came the casinos with poker rooms. These were mostly throughout California (particularly the Los Angeles area) and Las Vegas. But the big deal was that there was competition, so you could find the best game within a cardroom or you could take a short drive to a different cardroom. Sometimes you could still play in private games. That meant a lot more choices than when Amarillo Slim, Puggy Pearson, Sailor Roberts, I and others chased games around the South.

But, now—with online poker—a small- or medium-limit player has hundreds of games to choose from. There are usually ample choices within a single online cardroom, and some players choose never to go elsewhere. But, if you want to, you can open accounts at a multitude of online sites, so you can find the best game for either making money or enjoying yourself.

ONLINE POKER TIP #6
PRACTICE AT SMALLER STAKES

One of the great advantages of online play is that you'll get to practice heads-up no-limit and other rare games at smaller stakes that are generally not available in real-world casinos.

You should take advantage of this opportunity to explore these games economically.

ONLINE POKER TIP #7
LEVERAGE THE BLIND POSITIONS

An important thing happens to the blinds when the game becomes heads-up: The big blind acts after the small blind, and both blinds act after the dealer button.

Years ago the button position was usually the big blind and the other player took the small blind. But this gave too little incentive for the non-button player to enter the pot so the situation was reversed: The button would take the small blind and the opponent would have more reason to play, having already wagered twice as much.

Now, if one player sits out, what happens? Here's how it looks when only two players compete:

Notice that only the player at the upper right and far-left are competing for this pot and that the player in the top middle is sitting out. Now, the small blind is no longer to the left of the button. The button takes on the role of the small blind and the opponent has the big blind.

This means the dealer position must act before the big blind when playing heads up. There's an important tip associated with this: In a ring game, you should some-times leverage your position against the small blind by reraising with hands that are mediocre. I'll often do that in the big blind with hands such as A-6, K-10 or Q-J. These seem like calling hands, not raising ones, but be-cause I'll have position over the small blind on all the betting rounds, this raise often makes sense. I'm hoping that my opponent will just call pre-flop and then check to me after the flop.

If I make a hand or think I have a bluffing opportu-nity, I'll then go ahead and bet. But, if I end up with a flop where I'd rather take a free card, I can do that. It will be my choice, because I took an aggressive stance with position before the flop.

But, heads-up, it's different. You seldom should make those extra-aggressive raises when you don't have posi-tion. By modern conventions, the blinds are reversed and the big blind will have the *worst* position on all betting on the flop and beyond. The big blind needs to sacrifice some aggression in deference to the reality that he will act first and be at a disadvantage thereafter.

Position is something you need to consider, especially online, where there's less psychological warfare and raw strategy and position often dictate the right answer.

ONLINE POKER TIP #8
TAKING ADVANTAGE OF HASTY ACTIONS

Because your opponents tend to act so quickly online, I believe they give less consideration to the proper decisions. They simply act too swiftly—wham, bam! They tend to be caught up in the moment and act impulsively.

What does that mean to you? For one thing, I find that you can let players hang themselves more frequently online. If they get a mind to bluff, you can check and let them wager for you on every betting round. In traditional poker games, I'm much more likely to take the lead and bet into weak players. But, online, once I've checked and been bet into, I'll often just keep checking.

It's a rhythm. The action is so fast that you can check and an opponent will make another bad bet into you without thinking. You call fast. The next card is dealt electronically and instantly, and you call again. Only on the river—assuming your hand is powerful enough—do you raise.

Online, many opponents tend to keep bluffing once they've begun and to keep "value betting" weak hands. It's all in the pace. It happens so quickly that they don't re-evaluate as readily as they do in physical games. In traditional games, players take more time to think. Online, they tend to act instinctively more that rationally.

This gives you an opportunity to let players get themselves in trouble by checking and calling—and not raising until the last betting round *if* you have the strength to justify it.

As an example, suppose you're in the big blind with...

And you call a middle position raiser. Now the flop comes...

I might bet, but online against quick-acting, impulsive opponents, I'll usually check my three nines. There's apt to be a bet and I'll just call. A raise would set off alarm bells within an opponent's head.

I don't recommend that type of play in real-world casinos, except as an occasional alternative way of playing a hand. But, online, I recommend that you use that tactic regularly against those who get trapped in the excitement and fail to re-evaluate in the course of a hand.

That type of player will keep betting and betting. And all you need to do is keep calling and calling. They'll hang themselves, but mercifully for them, they'll do it quickly—without hesitation.

ONLINE POKER TIP #9
SACRIFICE MARGINAL HANDS WHEN PLAYING MULTIPLE GAMES

So, what do you do when you're playing more than one game at the same time? Besides recognizing that you won't be able to concentrate fully on each game—getting a good feel for how each individual opponent is playing—there are some practical considerations.

First, there are many marginal hands that you can either choose to play or not play. When you're playing multiple games, you can sacrifice these hands. Just fold them. If you were in only one game, you would consider playing them, because it might help your image along a little or might actually earn a small profit in the long run.

But, online when you're playing more than one game, you probably should forget about developing a lively image. If you do, opponents are just likely to play back at you in imaginative ways and you'll have to concentrate even *more* on that game than you would otherwise. Unfortunately, because you're playing more than one game, you can't.

The other bad thing about playing marginal hands when you're involved in multiple games is that you would do worse than otherwise with your attention divided and instead, you'll probably lose money with them. Now, if these hands are no longer profitable, doesn't it make sense not to play them at all?

And there's another problem with playing marginal hands. When you're involved in a pot in one game with one of these hands, you're limited in how effectively you can play a pot in the *other* game.

So, in effect, you're playing a hand that can't win money overall in the one game *and* hurting your chances of winning in the other game. That's bad.

ONLINE POKER TIP #10
HANDS TO SACRIFICE WHEN PLAYING MULTIPLE GAMES: SHORT-HANDED ADVICE

Playing marginal hands is particularly bad if one or more games are short-handed. You'll be involved in multiple pots so often that you couldn't do justice to either game, unless you stick to a basic strategy and fold as many break-even hands as possible. If you don't believe me, try playing two or more heads-up games at once!

So, I'm advising you to either resist the urge to play multiple games or to be more selective about the hands you enter pots with.

Which hands, exactly, should you stop playing? I've given it some thought, and the following tips include a list of examples. There are more hands than this, but these are the *type* of hands you should sacrifice.

ONLINE POKER TIP #11
HANDS TO SACRIFICE WHEN PLAYING MULTIPLE SHORT-HANDED GAMES: EARLY POSITION

From early positions in a full-handed limit hold'em game, when no one else has come in, exclude hands such as the four shown here...

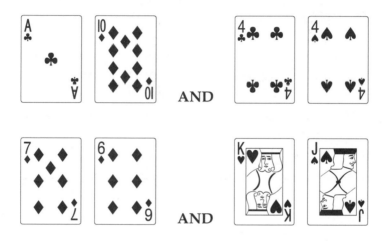

Online, you normally can play A-10 fairly early, because so many players come into the pot with weaker hands, even aces with very unattractive kickers. A-10 in a real-world game can often be dominated, especially against knowledgeable opponents, making it risky to enter the pot early with them. Online it's usually flat out profitable to come in with the hand early, but not by much. So, when you're playing more than one game at once, fold it. Remember, you're not just avoiding having to play that hand, you're giving yourself a chance to concentrate on the *other* game for a few precious seconds.

Small pairs tend to just break even or make a tiny profit from early positions, *if* you can fully concentrate. Since you usually can't when you're playing two or more games, these are easy fold candidates.

Likewise, small suited connectors, such as the 7-6 of diamonds are often near break-even hands and can be folded.

One of the easiest folds from an early position when you're playing multiple games online is K-J offsuit. In real-world games, this is seldom profitable. And online, it is often unprofitable, too. While you can pick and choose your spots to play, it only makes sense when you can concentrate fully on just that one game. Then it might be close to break even against the right group of opponents. But, it's such a dangerous hand that you need to be a superior player facing very weak opponents to make a profit with it. And when you're playing more than one game, you can't be a superior-enough player. So, fold that, too.

ONLINE POKER TIP #12
HANDS TO SACRIFICE WHEN PLAYING MULTIPLE SHORT-HANDED GAMES: MIDDLE POSITION

From middle positions in a full-handed limit hold'em game, when no one else has come in, exclude hands such as the following four examples...

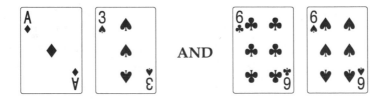

 AND

The kicker trouble with the ace when you're holding A-3 makes it just too difficult to play when you can't concentrate fully on the hand, even against loose online opponents.

The other hands aren't profitable for the same reasons as stated earlier. You can obviously play more hands in the middle positions than in the earliest positions, but again, you should play fewer hands than otherwise because you cannot fully concentrate on just the one game.

ONLINE POKER TIP #13
HANDS TO SACRIFICE WHEN PLAYING MULTIPLE SHORT-HANDED GAMES: LATE POSITION

From late positions—including the button—in a full-handed limit hold'em game, when no one else has come in, exclude hands like...

  AND

Of course, the decision to play these hands depends on your exact position and other game factors, but the point remains—these marginal hands are better folded so that you can concentrate better on the other game.

ONLINE POKER TIP #14
HANDS TO SACRIFICE WHEN PLAYING MULTIPLE SHORT-HANDED GAMES: SMALL BLIND

From the small blind position in a full-handed limit hold'em game, when no one else has come in, exclude hands like the four shown here...

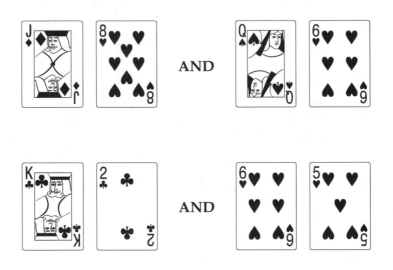

These hands are just not worth the effort, because they cost too much in mental demands and pay too little in profit when you're trying to tackle two or more games.

The K-2 of clubs may seem tempting to play, because of the added flush possibility, but it just doesn't account for enough extra profit to make it worthwhile. The same goes for the 6-5 of hearts.

Note that you might play all of those hands against the majority of big-blind opponents if you were focusing on just one game.

ONLINE POKER TIP #15
HANDS TO SACRIFICE WHEN PLAYING MULTIPLE SHORT-HANDED GAMES: BIG BLIND

From the big blind in a full-handed limit hold'em game, when an early or middle position has raised, exclude the following hands unless there are at least two opponents...

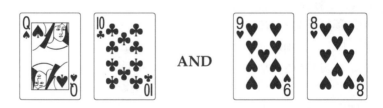

Also, exclude hands such as the following:

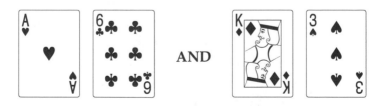

When a late position or small blind player has raised, exclude hands like...

 AND

**Summary of Playing Marginal
Hands in Multiple Games**

These are only examples of the types of hands you can exclude when you're in multiple games, not a complete list. But they should serve well to illustrate the point.

ONLINE POKER TIP #16
PAY MORE ATTENTION
TO THE BIGGER GAMES

This should go without saying, but I'm guessing many players are in violation of this rule: *If you're playing two or more games at once of different sizes, pay more attention to the bigger games.*

The game that promises to provide the most profit or threatens the potential of greater loss is the one you should pay more attention to. Don't put yourself in a situation where you're focusing so much on trying to maximize your profit with a big hand in a small game, that you make mistakes in the larger one.

This is equally true if you're playing online in a tournament and a regular poker game at the same time. At early stages in the tournament, the consequences of a mistake may not be so important, so you should probably put a lot of focus on the real-money game, especially if it's sizeable. But, as you get toward the conclusion of the tournament, that becomes more important and you should either quit the regular game—which is what I recommend—or put most of your focus on the tournament.

And if you're simultaneously playing two tournaments of the same size, obviously you should concentrate more on the one where you're closer to the money.

ONLINE POKER TIP #17
CHECK TO SEE IF OPPONENTS ARE PLAYING MULTIPLE GAMES

Since you can browse other games while you're playing, it's a good idea to check to see if any of your opponents are at other tables. If they are, you can make certain assumptions about how they'll play.

For example, players who are in multiple games are more likely to just call and less likely to bluff—unless they're already involved in a pot. They're also less likely to make sophisticated plays from the get-go. So, adjust your strategy with that in mind.

ONLINE POKER TIP #18
OPPONENTS EARLY ACTION CHOICES

There is something I find useful about pre-select buttons. They can provide tells. Watch the speed with which someone acts. If a decision is pre-selected, then it usually will occur instantly when the action reaches that player.

I say "usually," because the occasional lapses in Internet communications mean that sometimes there will be a delay, even if the action has already been chosen and the software is trying to respond immediately. Most of the time this delay won't happen, and you can get some information because of opponents' use of these special buttons.

The main thing I keep in my head is that when an action happens instantly, it's probably a result of a pre-selected action. Why would an opponent pre-select? There's only one reason I can think of. That opponent knows that he's going to take that action, no matter what anyone else does in front of him. That puts an added emphasis to that opponent's decision, in my mind.

For example, what if no bet is due and an opponent instantly checks? Chances are, the player has determined in advance that he is going to check. At Doyle's Room, he may have selected either the "Check/Fold" button, which is a typical choice, or the lesser-used "Check/Call any" button. It is probable that the "Check/Fold" was chosen, and, if that's so, then I can assume that the instant check means the player likely would have automatically folded if there had been a bet and I'll give the player less credit for having a strong hand.

Other Tells

Similarly, if an opponent raises instantly, I'm pretty sure he intended to raise no matter what, and that usually indicates a very strong hand.

There are other tells you can divine from these pre-select buttons, when you take the time to think about what an instant action means. If an opponent seems to frequently use the pre-select buttons, but occasionally hesitates, you can figure him for a type of hand where the decision is not obvious. So, always consider what an instant action—or the lack of one—might mean.

ONLINE POKER TIP #19
OTHERS MIGHT BE WATCHING YOUR EARLY ACTION CHOICES

Sometimes you can get clues to your opponents' hands through their use of early action buttons. But, I always remember that if I'm trying to improve my decisions by taking this factor into consideration, a few of my most sophisticated opponents might be doing the same thing. They might be trying to gain information by reading *my* early action choices!

Now, I'm used to players trying to read me in traditional poker games. They've been trying to do it since my earliest days. But, I've always been careful not to reveal the strength of my hand to them. I deliberately bet the same way most times, and I avoid projecting tells. Mostly my goal in these face-to-face poker games is to avoid being read. And I'm proud of my success at it. But, online I might be read, just because I chose an early action and the software announced my decision so quickly when it became my turn that it was apparent I had planned that action no matter what.

To avoid being read as having a weak hand in the big blind, for instance, because my instant let's-see-the-flop call looks like I clicked the "Check or Fold" button, I'll sometimes use the "Check or Call" early action button when I'm in the big blind with a higher quality hand. If nobody raises, this will throw players who are looking for this clue off the trail. Since I'm occasionally going to just call with a big hand, just for deception, why not incorporate an early action button into that decision?

Now, my observant opponents might incorrectly interpret that to mean I called weakly in the big blind and would have folded had there been a raise. Actually, I had clicked a button instructing the software to just check my big hand and see the flop if nobody raised *and* to call the bet if somebody did raise. Players have the tendency, I believe, to assume that a quick, let's-see-the-flop check is more likely to mean that the player would have folded had there been a raise than to mean that the player would have called. But, in either case, your opponent isn't likely to think that you have a big hand that you could have raised with—but you do!

You can, of course, wait until the action reaches your seat before you decide how you will act on a hand.

More on the Early Action Buttons

It is sometime valuable to call with a big hand—which you'd do anyway—for the sake of deception. And you'll be setting the hook even deeper into those few observant opponents who misinterpret the instant call as a tell that you don't have a strong hand.

There are other uses of the early action buttons that can defeat the plans of opponents to read you. My point is this: You should mix-up the use of early action buttons, just as you would mix up the use of your call/raise and other choices in traditional physical games.

ONLINE POKER TIP #20
QUICK VERSUS INSTANT DECISIONS

Often it's difficult to tell the difference between a player who clicked quickly and one who used a pre-select button. The difference matters, though, even though both responses come to you quickly. If a pre-select button was used, the decision was probably obvious no matter what other players did. If it's just a quick last-second response, it may be that the decision is obvious now, but it might have been less obvious and taken more time had the other players acted differently.

For instance, Jack may be holding J-8 offsuit in late position. He's apt to wait to see what to do. If an opponent also in late position just calls the blind, Jack may call quickly, but not instantly. Calling isn't usually the right play in this case, but many of your opponents will do it, as long as nobody in an early seat played. If Jack had a slightly better hand with straight-flush possibilities, such as J-10 suited, he is likely to press a pre-selected call button. In that case, you'll see an instant call. It will appear to you as if both players called at once.

Learn to recognize the difference between this pre-selected, instant action and one where a player acted quickly, but left a slight hesitation between his decision and the one preceding.

ONLINE POKER TIP #21
BETS THAT THREATEN

Just as in the real-world, immediate bets and raises—those made without hesitation—are the most threatening and the least likely to indicate a bluff. This tell is even more pronounced online, where players are clicking their buttons eagerly when their choice is certain. Bluffing usually takes a little time to consider, even if it's just a second.

On the other hand, beware of a *long* hesitation. That can be a deliberate attempt by an opponent holding a strong hand to make you think he is undecided.

To sum this up, beware of both immediate bets *and* bets made after a long delay. Anything in between is more worthy of a call.

ONLINE POKER TIP #22
EARLY TOURNAMENT STRATEGY

There is more than one theory about how to play early in an online tournament. But I believe there's just no reason to risk getting knocked out in the first round.

I'll usually take a few stabs at a pot, maybe leveraging a hand or even bluffing, but in either case, I won't get much money involved. I think this philosophy is especially wise online, because many players move all-in too recklessly. This all-in tactic might sound like an easy road to profit, but in truth, you're going to be tempted to move all-in yourself with only a small advantage—which is not a good idea. Yes, it can be profitable, but you risk getting busted out with a hand that just didn't warrant that kind of risk. There's more profit in letting the loosest players attack each other and reduce the field. Early in a tournament, you can afford to wait for a major advantage before committing a large share of your chips or even all of them.

What usually happens early in an online tournament is that some weak players will double up or even increase their chip stacks by more than that, while many other reckless players get eliminated early. I try to survive and build gradually during the early rounds. If I get a hand to go to war with, I will. But, unless that happens, I'm just not willing to get knocked out early.

The most successful strategy I know is to survive and to build gradually through small pots until the cards give you the opportunity to win big. There's no rush—in online or in real-world tournaments.

Later in the tournament, the stakes will get so big in comparison to the chips on the table that you'll have to gamble. You'll have to take chances sometimes, even be a little reckless and hope for the best. But my advice is not to do that until you must.

ONLINE POKER TIP #23
TRUST IN YOUR ONLINE ROOM

You need to play at an online cardroom that you trust to pay you. If you're worried about getting paid if you win, you're in the worst kind of situation and I'd advise you to find a place to play where you're more comfortable.

In years past, I've felt uncomfortable playing at some cardrooms and in home games for that matter, and have felt comfortable playing in other environments. No doubt, the same will be true for you with online poker rooms.

One thing I learned a long time ago is to play poker when it feels right and walk away—sometimes run away—when it doesn't. It doesn't mean there's anything wrong with the game or the casino you choose to avoid, but the mere fact that you're not comfortable means you can't concentrate on playing your most profitable game. You're naturally worried about other things. You've got enough to think about when you're playing poker to win, without having to add psychological agonies—real or imagined.

ONLINE POKER TIP #24
SIT AND GO STRATEGY

Sit-and-goes can get to be a habit in a hurry—and a very profitable one for accomplished players. The trick is to play a solid game, trying to survive and share in one of the three payouts—for first, second, or third. As much as my temperament tells me to always go for first place, this really isn't the best strategy in these one-table shootouts, where nobody keeps track of your "championships." It's better to play a more conservative game than you would in a regular ring game. You should play a little more selectively, trying to survive until there are just two players left and then open up.

The same is true of all online tournaments where you play down to a few players who share the prize money. You won't have the same psychological opportunities to conquer opponents as you would in real-world games, so the proven best choice is to play more solidly.

ONLINE POKER TIP #25
LEARN MORE GAMES

My advice is that you should specialize in hold'em and pretty much stick to that during your online familiarization process. That's the game where most of the potential for online profit is, simply because there are so many tables of hold'em that you can be more picky about the ones you join.

However, just because you should specialize in hold'em online doesn't mean you shouldn't be prepared to play other games, as well. You never know where the most profitable games will be at a given time, and you can't take advantage if you haven't learned how to play productively in other games besides hold'em. Sure, you could get by fine online without ever playing anything but hold'em. But, if you want to have a shot at the most profit possible, you should eventually learn to play all the games proficiently.

Although seven-card stud, Omaha, Omaha high-low (eight-or-better), and old-fashioned draw poker won't likely take up a great deal of your time online, you'll want to investigate them further when you get the chance. You never know when somebody with a lot of money to unload will waltz into one of those games.

And it would be a shame if you didn't know enough to take advantage of the opportunity.

Loose Ends
&
Closing
Comments

The Internet has changed the world, and it's rein-vented poker. Besides the obvious advantages that will draw new players to our game, allowing them to learn the game by playing just for fun or for very small stakes, there are subtle developments that might not immediately come to mind.

For the first time, we now have a good idea which hands make money in which positions. We know this because analysis is beginning to be published about how actual hands fared online. Mike Caro compiled the first such study in 2000 and other sites and researchers have been contributing to this body of knowledge ever since.

I'll be eager to see the many examinations of results that are sure to follow. But one thing is for certain: This could never have happened without the advent of online poker. How else is anyone going to chronicle the results of millions of actual poker hands? Today it can be done automatically, without identifying specific players. This general understanding of how hands fare is sure to be useful to those who play poker professionally or are just fascinated by the game.

HOW TO LEARN MORE

I've tried to give you a lot to think about in this book. In addition to the tips contained about general poker herein, consider exploring some of the remarkable books that have been written on poker. I recommend you pick up both my books *Super/System* (the original) and *Super/System 2* (the sequel). You might also want to explore the psychological aspect of the game more deeply in *Caro's Book of Poker Tells* and if you're in Las Vegas, visit Gambler's Book Shop to select a more complete library, or go online to Cardoza Publishing's website, www.cardozapub.com, for a complete selection of their diverse library of poker titles.

Be sure to visit DoylesRoom.com or DoylesRoom.net for links to constantly updated poker material. We have an exclusive arrangement with Mike Caro University of Poker and Poker1.com, and you're apt to be very pleasantly surprised at the free offerings we'll be providing there.

To have your best shot at being a winning online poker player, I have summarized 10 key tips that are important. Let's take a look at them now.

10 KEY TIPS TO WINNING ONLINE

KEY TIP # 1.

It doesn't matter how much you know if you don't use the knowledge wisely. So make wise choices to extract the best profits possible.

KEY TIP # 2.

Have patience. There's never been a man or woman who could beat poker without it. If you sit down just to have fun, that's fine. There's nothing wrong with playing poker purely for recreation, but don't expect to win in the long run.

KEY TIP # 3.

Don't try to play too fancy online. Most of those superior people-reading skills that might work for you in the real world won't work online. You need to just accept the fact that players aren't paying as much attention to you personally and won't be as intimidated by you as much as they might be if you were physically present. That means the best advice I can give you in this regard is to just play your cards the way they fall. Don't try to force something to happen if the cards don't support you. You can sometimes power your way through a real-world game without cards, but online, you'll find it much more difficult. So, again, play your cards.

KEY TIP # 4.

Remember that in the absence of physical tells, you won't be able to scrutinize your opponents. Again, this means that you'll have fewer opportunities to be creative by adapting to your opponents' moods and mannerisms. Online, the answer is to play using more straightforward strategy and use less psychology.

KEY TIP # 5.

Don't put too much emphasis on the few online tells we've talked about. Remember, these mostly involve the use of pre-select buttons. Instant actions generally mean clear decisions were made without waiting to see what opponents would do, but keep in mind, that this can be misleading. A slight delay in communication across the Internet can lead you to believe a player hesitated when he actually did use a pre-select button.

KEY TIP # 6.

The best tell is probably the use of the Check-Fold button. When you see a player check instantly after waiting for two or more players to act, it's likely that the button was used. If it was, it means the hand wasn't good enough to call a bet with, so you can sometimes eliminate strong starting hands as possibilities in the later betting rounds.

KEY TIP # 7.

It can be difficult to recognize the subtle difference between an opponent who called or checked using a pre-select button and one who acted quickly at the last moment. But, you should learn to recognize this difference. It can help you speculate more accurately about what your opponent might hold. A pre-selected choice often will appear as if two players acted almost at once.

KEY TIP # 8.

You need to guard your bankroll a little more closely online, because it takes more effort to get money back onto the tables if you go broke. You can't just take it out of your pocket; you must go through the process of electronically transferring funds to your account before you can buy more chips. Although some sites allow you to lend money to other players, Doyle's Room and most other online poker rooms don't. I think that preventing loans to fellow players on online sites is a good thing, because it prevents constant begging and harassment from players who have gone dry and takes the pressure off players who still have chips. It gives them an excuse not to lend money at poker. And the excuse is simple—*they can't.*

KEY TIP # 9.

You might be able to keep players from reading you by trying to take about the same amount of time to act, no matter what. Just don't make it a long delay—that's discourteous to other players.

KEY TIP # 10.

Use all the professional techniques you've learned in this book, but keep it simple whenever possible. That's the purest path to online poker profit.

Of course, those are just a few reminders of the many things we've discussed in this book. The important tip is to have fun online. Internet poker wasn't intended to become your whole life. It is only offered to add another exciting dimension to your life. But, what an exciting new dimension it is!

MY FINAL THOUGHTS

Now we all have computers, and they do almost everything for us. Poker is just an extension of that "almost everything." I know players who use a laptop computer to play poker, propped up against a pillow in their beds. And some play using wireless connections from airports when waiting for their next plane.

It used to be pretty hard to get a game together if you weren't near a public casino. But now the games are always there, almost anywhere in the world, 24 hours a day, everyday. Always.

I'm still partial to the type of poker I grew up with, face-to-face poker, where you can stare a man down, open a window into his emotions and his character, and crush him by pure force of will. Until we advance to the stage where you're looking at your opponents via webcam or whatever—and I expect that will happen soon—we'll have to sacrifice some of poker's person-to-person charm. Still, I've grown to love the game online. It's just so easy to get to a game and so fast-paced that I quickly seem content and forget about the tells and the people skills I'm not able to use.

POKER IS POKER

In many ways, it's still the same poker online. And in many ways, it's much better, as I've shown you in these pages. It all comes down to one pure truth about poker. Poker *is* poker. Wherever you play it, there's only one game like it.

Come visit me at www.doylesroom.com. Hope to see you online!

THE CHAMPIONSHIP SERIES
POWERFUL BOOKS YOU MUST HAVE

CHAMPIONSHIP OMAHA (Omaha High-Low, Pot-limit Omaha, Limit High Omaha) by Tom McEvoy & T.J. Cloutier. Clearly-written strategies and powerful advice from Cloutier and McEvoy who have won four World Series of Poker titles in Omaha tournaments. Powerful advice shows you how to win at low-limit and high-stakes games, how to play against loose and tight opponents, and the differing strategies for rebuy and freezeout tournaments. Learn the best starting hands, when slowplaying a big hand is dangerous, what danglers are and why winners don't play them, why pot-limit Omaha is the only poker game where you sometimes fold the nuts on the flop and are correct in doing so and overall, and how you can win a lot of money at Omaha! 296 pages, photos, illustrations, New Edition! $29.95!

CHAMPIONSHIP STUD (Seven-Card Stud, Stud 8/or Better and Razz) by Dr. Max Stern, Linda Johnson, and Tom McEvoy. The authors, who have earned millions of dollars in major tournaments and cash games, eight World Series of Poker bracelets and hundreds of other titles in competition against the best players in the world show you the winning strategies for medium-limit side games as well as poker tournaments and a general tournament strategy that is applicable to any form of poker. Includes give-and-take conversations between the authors to give you more than one point of view on how to play poker. 200 pages, hand pictorials, photos. $39.95.

CHAMPIONSHIP HOLD'EM by Tom McEvoy & T.J. Cloutier. Hard-hitting hold'em the way it's played today in both limit cash games and tournaments. Get killer advice on how to win more money in rammin'-jammin' games, kill-pot, jackpot, shorthanded, and other types of cash games. You'll learn the thinking process before the flop, on the flop, on the turn, and at the river with specific suggestions for what to do when good or bad things happen plus 20 illustrated hands with play-by-play analyses. Specific advice for rocks in tight games, weaklings in loose games, experts in solid games, how hand values change in jackpot games, when you should fold, check, raise, reraise, check-raise, slowplay, bluff, and tournament strategies for small buy-in, big buy-in, rebuy, incremental add-on, satellite and big-field major tournaments. Wow! Easy-to-read and conversational, if you want to become a lifelong winner at limit hold'em, you need this book! 388 Pages, Illustrated, Photos. ~~$39.95~~. Now only $29.95!

CHAMPIONSHIP NO-LIMIT & POT-LIMIT HOLD'EM by T.J. Cloutier & Tom McEvoy. New Cardoza Edition! The definitive guide to winning at two of the world's most exciting poker games! Written by eight time World Champion players T.J. Cloutier (1998 and 2002 Player of the Year) and Tom McEvoy (the foremost author on tournament strategy) who have won millions of dollars each playing no-limit and pot-limit hold'em in cash games and major tournaments around the world. You'll get all the answers here—no holds barred—to your most important questions: How do you get inside your opponents' heads and learn how to beat them at their own game? How can you tell how much to bet, raise, and reraise in no-limit hold'em? When can you bluff? How do you set up your opponents in pot-limit hold'em so you can win a monster pot? What are the best strategies for winning no-limit and pot-limit tournaments, satellites, and supersatellites? You get rock-solid and inspired advice from two of the most recognizable figures in poker—advice that you can bank on. If you want to become a winning player, and a champion, you must have this book. 304 pages, paperback, illustrations, photos. $29.95

THE CHAMPIONSHIP SERIES
POWERFUL BOOKS YOU MUST HAVE

CHAMPIONSHIP TOURNAMENT POKER by Tom McEvoy. New Cardoza Edition! Rated by pros as best book on tournaments ever written and enthusiastically endorsed by more than five world champions, this is the definitive guide to winning tournaments and a must for every player's library. McEvoy lets you in on the secrets he has used to win millions of dollars in tournaments and the insights he has learned competing against the best players in the world. Packed solid with winning strategies for all 11 games in the World Series of Poker, with extensive discussions of 7-card stud, limit hold'em, pot and no-limit hold'em, Omaha high-low, re-buy, half-half tournaments, satellites, and strategies for each stage of tournaments. Tons of essential concepts and specific strategies jam-pack the book. Phil Hellmuth, 1989 WSOP champion says, "[this] is the world's most definitive guide to winning poker tournaments." 416 pages, paperback, $29.95.

CHAMPIONSHIP TABLE (at the World Series of Poker) by Dana Smith, Ralph Wheeler, and Tom McEvoy. New Cardoza Edition! From 1970 when the champion was presented a silver cup, to the present when the champion was awarded more than $2 million, *Championship Table* celebrates three decades of poker greats who have competed to win poker's most coveted title. This book gives you the names and photographs of all the players who made the final table, pictures of the last hand the champion played against the runner-up, how they played their cards, and how much they won. This book also features fascinating interviews and conversations with the champions and runners-up and interesting highlights from each Series. This is a fascinating and invaluable resource book for WSOP and gaming buffs. In some cases the champion himself wrote "how it happened," as did two-time champion Doyle Brunson when Stu Ungar caught a wheel in 1980 on the turn to deprive "Texas Dolly" of his third title. Includes tons of vintage photographs. 208 pages, paperback, $19.95.

CHAMPIONSHIP WIN YOUR WAY INTO BIG MONEY HOLD'EM TOURNAMENTS by Brad Daugherty & Tom McEvoy. In 2003 and 2004, satellite players won their way into the $10,000 WSOP buy-in and emerged as champions, winning more than $2 million each. You can too! You'll learn specific, proven strategies for winning almost any satellite. Learn the ten ways to win a seat at the WSOP and other big tournaments, how to win limit hold'em and no-limit hold'em satellites, one-table satellites for big tournaments, and online satellites, plus how to play the final table of super satellites. McEvoy and Daugherty sincerely believe that if you practice these strategies, you can win your way into any tournament for a fraction of the buy-in. You'll learn how much to bet, how hard to pressure opponents, how to tell when an opponent is bluffing, how to play deceptively, and how to use your chips as weapons of destruction. Includes a special chapter on no-limit hold'em satellites! 320 pages. Illustrated hands, photos, glossary. $29.95.

CHAMPIONSHIP HOLD'EM TOURNAMENT HANDS by T.J. Cloutier & Tom McEvoy. Two tournament legends show you how to become a winning tournament player. Get inside their heads as they think their way through the correct strategy at 57 limit and no-limit practice hands. Cloutier and McEvoy show you how to use your skill and intuition to play strategic hands for maximum profit in real tournament scenarios and how 45 key hands were played by champions in turnaround situations at the WSOP. By sharing their analysis on how the winners and losers played key hands, you'll gain tremendous insights into how tournament poker is played at the highest levels. Learn how champions think and how they play major hands in strategic tournament situations, Cloutier and McEvoy believe that you will be able to win your share of the profits in today's tournaments—and join them at the championship table far sooner than you ever imagined. 368 pages, illustrated with card pictures, $29.95

FROM CARDOZA'S EXCITING LIBRARY
ADD THESE TO YOUR COLLECTION - ORDER NOW!

POKER WISDOM OF A CHAMPION by Doyle Brunson. Learn what it takes to be a great poker player by climbing inside the mind of poker's most famous champion. Fascinating anecdotes and adventures from Doyle's early career playing poker in roadhouses and with other great champions are interspersed with important lessons you can learn from the champion who has made more money at poker than anyone else in the history of the game. You'll learn what makes a great player tick, how he approaches the game, and receive candid, powerful advice from the legend himself. The Mad Genius of poker, Mike Caro, says, "Brunson is the greatest poker player who ever lived. This book shows why." 192 pages. $14.95.

CARO'S BOOK OF POKER TELLS by Mike Caro. The classic book is now revised and back in print! This long-awaited brand new edition by the Mad Genius of Poker, takes a detailed look at the art and science of tells, the physical giveaways by players on their hands. Featuring photos of poker players in action along with Caro's explanations about when players are bluffing and when they're not. These powerful eye-opening ideas can give you the decisive edge at the table! This invaluable book should be in every player's library! 320 pages. $24.95.

KEN WARREN TEACHES TEXAS HOLD'EM by Ken Warren. This is a step-by-step comprehensive manual for making money at hold'em poker. 42 powerful chapters will teach you one lesson at a time. Great practical advice and concepts with examples from actual games and how to apply them to your own play. Lessons include: Starting Cards, Playing Position, Which Hands to Play, Raising, Check-raising, Tells, Game/Seat Selection, Dominated Hands, Odds, and much more. This book is already a huge fan favorite and best-seller! 416 pages. $26.95.

WINNERS GUIDE TO TEXAS HOLD'EM POKER by Ken Warren. The most powerful book on beating hold'em shows serious players how to play every hand from every position with every type of flop. Learn the 14 categories of starting hands, the 10 most common hold'em tells, how to evaluate a game for profit, value of deception, art of bluffing, eight secrets to winning, starting hand categories, position, and more! Bonus: Includes detailed analysis of the top 40 hands and the most complete chapter on hold'em odds in print. Over 500,000 copies in print. 224 pages. $16.95.

THE BIG BOOK OF POKER by Ken Warren. This easy-to-read and oversized guide teaches you everything you need to know to win money at home poker, in cardrooms, casinos and on the tournament circuit. Readers will learn how to bet, raise, and checkraise, bluff, semi-bluff, and how to take advantage of position and pot odds. Great sections on hold'em (plus, stud games, Omaha, draw games, and many more) and playing and winning poker on the internet. Packed with charts, diagrams, sidebars, and detailed, easy-to-read examples by best-selling poker expert Ken Warren, this wonderfully formatted book is one stop shopping for players ready to take on any form of poker for real money. Want to be a big player? Buy the *Big Book of Poker*! 320 oversized pages. $19.95.

HOW TO PLAY WINNING POKER by Avery Cardoza. New and expanded edition shows playing and winning strategies for all major games: 5 and 7-stud games, Omaha, draw poker, hold'em, and high-low, both for home and casino play. You'll learn 15 winning poker concepts, how to minimize losses and maximize profits, how to read opponents and gain the edge against their style, how to use use pot odds, tells, position, more. 160 pages. $12.95.

Order Toll-Free 1-800-577-WINS or www.cardozapub.com

FROM CARDOZA'S EXCITING LIBRARY
ADD THESE TO YOUR COLLECTION - ORDER NOW!

COWBOYS, GAMBLERS & HUSTLERS: The True Adventures of a Rodeo Champion & Poker Legend by Byron "Cowboy" Wolford. Ride along with the road gamblers as they fade the white line from Dallas to Shreveport to Houston in the 1960s in search of a score. Feel the fear and frustration of being hijacked, getting arrested for playing poker, and having to outwit card sharps and scam artists. Wolford survived it all to win a WSOP gold bracelet playing with poker greats Amarillo Slim Preston, Johnny Moss and Bobby Baldwin (and 30 rodeo belt buckles). Read fascinating yarns about life on the rough and tumble, and colorful adventures as a road gambler and hustler gambling in smoky backrooms with legends Titanic Thompson, Jack Straus, Doyle Brunson and get a look at vintage Las Vegas when Cowboy's friend, Benny Binion ruled Glitter Gulch. Read about the most famous bluff in WSOP history. Endorsed by Jack Binion, Doyle Brunson and Bobby Baldwin, who says, Cowboy is probably the best gambling story teller in the world. 304 pages, $19.95.

SECRETS OF WINNING POKER by Tex Sheahan. This is a compilation of Sheahan's best articles from 15 years of writing for the major gaming magazines as his legacy to poker players. Sheahan gives you sound advice on winning poker strategies for hold'em and 7-card stud. Chapters on tournament play, psychology, personality profiles and some very funny stories from the greenfelt jungle. "Some of the best advice you'll ever read on how to win at poker" --Doyle Brunson. 200 pages, paperback. $19.95.

OMAHA HI-LO: Play to Win with the Odds by Bill Boston. Selecting the right hands to play is the most important decision you'll make in Omaha high-low poker. In this book you'll find the odds for every hand dealt in Omaha high-low—the chances that the hand has of winning the high end of the pot, the low end of it, and how often it is expected to scoop the whole pot. The results are based on 10,000 simulations for each one of the possible 5,211 Omaha high-low hands. Boston has organized the data into an easy-to-use format and added insights learned from years of experience. Learn the 5,211 Omaha high-low hands, the 49 best hands and their odds, the 49 worst hands, trap hands to avoid, and 30 Ace-less hands you can play for profit. A great tool for Omaha players! 156 pages, $19.95.

OMAHA HI-LO POKER (8 OR BETTER): How to win at the lower limits by Shane Smith. Since its first printing in 1991, this has become the classic in the field for low-limit players. Readers have lauded the author's clear and concise writing style. Smith shows you how to put players on hands, read the board for high and low, avoid dangerous draws, and use winning betting strategies. Chapters include starting hands, the flop, the turn, the river, and tournament strategy. Illustrated with pictorials of sample hands, an odds chart, and a starting hands chart. Lou Krieger, author of *Poker for Dummies*, says, Shane Smith's book is terrific! If you're new to Omaha high-low split or if you're a low-limit player who wants to improve your game, you ought to have this book in your poker library. Complex concepts are presented in an easy-to-understand format. It's a gem! 82 pages, spiralbound. $17.95.

THE WACKY SIDE OF POKER by Ralph E. Wheeler. Take a walk on the wacky side with 88 humorous poker cartoons! Also includes 220 wise and witty poker quotes. Lighten up from all the heavy reading and preparation of the games with a quick walk through this fun book. Perfect for a holiday gift. 176 pages filled with wit and wisdom will bring a smile to your face. At less than a ten-spot, you can't go wrong! 176 pages, $11.95.

POWERFUL POKER SIMULATIONS

A MUST FOR SERIOUS PLAYERS WITH A COMPUTER!
IBM compatibles CD ROM Win 95, 98, 2000, NT, ME, XP - Full Color Graphics

These incredible full color poker simulation programs are the absolute best method to improve your game. Computer opponents play like real players. All games let you set the limits and rake, have fully programmable players, adjustable lineup, stat tracking, and Hand Analyzer for starting hands. MIke Caro, the world's foremost poker theoretician says, "Amazing...a steal for under $500...get it, it's great." Includes free telephone support. "Smart Advisor" gives expert advice for every play in every game!

NEW!
Windows Versions
More Features!

1. TURBO TEXAS HOLD'EM FOR WINDOWS - $89.95 - Choose which players, how many, 2-10, you want to play, create loose/tight game, control check-raising, bluffing, position, sensitivity to pot odds, more! Also, instant replay, pop-up odds, Professional Advisor, keeps track of play statistics. Free bonus: Hold'em Hand Analyzer analyzes all 169 pocket hands in detail, their win rates under any conditions you set. Caro says this "hold'em software is the most powerful ever created." Great product!

2. TURBO SEVEN-CARD STUD FOR WINDOWS - $89.95 - Create any conditions of play; choose number of players (2-8), bet amounts, fixed or spread limit, bring-in method, tight/loose conditions, position, reaction to board, number of dead cards, stack deck to create special conditions, instant replay. Terrific stat reporting includes analysis of starting cards, 3-D bar charts, graphs. Play interactively, run high speed simulation to test strategies. Hand Analyzer analyzes starting hands in detail. Wow!

3. TURBO OMAHA HIGH-LOW SPLIT FOR WINDOWS - $89.95 -Specify any playing conditions; betting limits, number of raises, blind structures, button position, aggressiveness/passiveness of opponents, number of players (2-10), types of hands dealt, blinds, position, board reaction, specify flop, turn, river cards! Choose opponents, use provided point count or create your own. Statistical reporting, instant replay, pop-up odds, high speed simulation to test strategies, amazing Hand Analyzer, much more!

4. TURBO OMAHA HIGH FOR WINDOWS - $89.95 - Same features as above, but tailored for Omaha High-only. Caro says program is "an electrifying research tool...it can clearly be worth thousands of dollars to any serious player. A must for Omaha High players.

5. TURBO 7 STUD 8 OR BETTER - $89.95 - Brand new with all the features you expect from the Wilson Turbo products: the latest artificial intelligence, instant advice and exact odds, play versus 2-7 opponents, enhanced data charts that can be exported or printed, the ability to fold out of turn and immediately go to the next hand, ability to peek at opponents hand, optional warning mode that warns you if a play disagrees with the advisor, and automatic testing mode that can run up to 50 tests unattended. Challenge tough computer players who vary their styles for a truly great poker game.

6. TOURNAMENT TEXAS HOLD'EM - $59.95

Set-up for tournament practice and play, this realistic simulation pits you against celebrity look-alikes. Tons of options let you control tournament size with 10 to 300 entrants, select limits, ante, rake, blind structures, freezeouts, number of rebuys and competition level of opponents - average, tough, or toughest. Pop-up status report shows how you're doing vs. the competition. Save tournaments in progress to play again later. Additional feature allows you to quickly finish a folded hand and go on to the next.

DOYLE BRUNSON'S SUPER SYSTEM 2
A COURSE IN POKER POWER!
by World Champion Doyle Brunson

Super System 2 gathers together the greatest players, theorists, and world champions and expands upon the original with more games, new authors, and most importantly, more professional secrets from the best in the business.

POKER'S GREATEST PLAYERS SHARE THEIR SECRETS

This superstar lineup is led by Doyle Brunson, two-time World Series of Poker Champion, nine-time WSOP gold bracelet winner, and the greatest poker player of all time. His hand-picked roster of expert collaborators includes: Daniel Negreanu, winner of multiple WSOP gold bracelets and 2004 Poker Player of the Year; Lyle Berman, three-time WSOP gold bracelet winner, founder of the World Poker Tour, and super-high stakes cash player; Bobby Baldwin, 1978 World Poker Champion and president of Bellagio; Johnny Chan, two-time World Poker Champion and nine-time WSOP gold bracelet winner; Mike Caro, poker's greatest researcher, theorist, and instructor; Jennifer Harman, the best female player in the history of poker and one of the ten best overall; Todd Brunson, winner of more than twenty tournaments; and Crandell Addington, a no-limit hold'em legend.

THE COMPLETE MASTERPIECE OF POKER

Together with the original *Super System*, hailed by professionals as the most influential book on poker ever written, this two-volume set comprises a full library of the best poker advice, strategies, and professional concepts ever published.

SERIOUS POKER PLAYERS MUST HAVE THIS BOOK

This is **mandatory reading** for aspiring poker pros, players planning to enter tournaments, and players ready to play no-limit. Doyle Brunson's *Super System 2* is also ideal for average players seeking to move to higher stakes games for more challenges and bigger wins.